Love,
Nawanna
Lewis
Miller

Oh God! My Preacher is Pregnant!

Oh God!

My Preacher is Pregnant!

"For anyone and everyone who ever dreams what seem to be impossible dreams or sees what seem to be impossible visions."

Nawanna Lewis Miller

B.A., M.A., M.Div.

Oh God! My Preacher is Pregnant!

Unless otherwise indicated, Scripture quotations are taken from the Kings James Version of the Holy Bible.

First Printing: December 5, 2017

Cover: Carey Germana – Graphic Design

Photo Credit: Nikko Tan/pexels.com - CC

ISBN-13:

Dedicated to the God of Jesus Christ

Who is Jehovah Perazim - The God of the Breakings Through!

(I Samuel 5:20; Isaiah 28:21)

To George C. Miller, Jr., my husband, our sons, our daughters, our grandsons, and all the generations of our children's children who shall come after, as long as our Lord shall tarry; the Reverend Dr. H. Beecher Hicks, Jr.; Dr. Elizabeth Hicks; Reverend Dr. Casey and LeeDonna Kimbrough; Reverend Dr. William E. and Lynn Harris; Reverend Patrick and Valerie Young; Reverend Donell Peterman; Reverend Robert Linden; the Clergy who embraced the boldness of Christ, Christ's mantle and Character to serve as my Council of Ordination for the Public Catechism and Ordination; Reverend Dr. Clarence Newsome; Reverend Dr. Kortright Davis; Reverend Dr. Cain Hope Felder; Reverend Dr. Evans Crawford; Reverend Dr. Alice Bellis; Reverend Dr. Cheryl Price; Reverend Brenda Girton Mitchell; Reverend Dr. Cynthia Turner; Reverend Dr. Maurice Watson; Oliver Kreitmann, MD; Kermit Simrel, MD; Metropolitan Baptist Church, Washington, D.C. and the Victorious Christian Living Bible Class; Elder Sarah Horne; Elder Georgia Whitted; all the saints who prayed for and encouraged us; and the 1500 saints of God who attended my Sacred Ordination.

In loving memory of our Parents; Ancestors; Reverend Dr. Julius C. Williams; Sergio Fabro, MD; Reverend Dr. H. Beecher Hicks, Sr. (Daddy Hicks); Reverend Dr. L. Charles Bennett; Reverend Dr. Marvis P. May; Reverend and Mrs. H. Wesley Wiley; Odean Horne, Sr.; Mrs. Gladiola McDaniel; and my Witness Cloud!

Deuteronomy 32:11-12

"As an eagle stirreth up her nest, flutters over her young, spreadeth abroad her wings, taketh them, beareth them on her wings: So the Lord alone did lead him, and there was no strange god with him."

Isaiah 40:28-31

"Hast thou not known? Hast thou not heard that the everlasting God, the Lord, the Creator of the ends of the earth, fainteth not, neither is weary? There is no searching of his understanding. He giveth power to the faint; and to them that have no might he increaseth strength. Even the youths shall faint and be weary, and the young men shall utterly fall: But they that wait upon the Lord shall renew their strength; they shall mount up with wings as eagles; they shall run, and not be weary; and they shall walk, and not faint."

Acts 2:17

"And it shall come to pass in the last days, saith God, I will pour out of my Spirit upon all flesh: and your sons and your daughters shall prophesy, and your young men shall see visions, and your old men shall dream dreams:"

Acts 2:18

"And on my servants and on my handmaidens I will pour out in those days of my Spirit; and they shall prophesy:"

Acts 21:9

"And the same man had four daughters, virgins, which did prophesy."

Chapter 1
Oh God!
My Heart Wants to Talk to You!

"Walk quietly into the exquisite
beauty
and perfect splendor of Eternal Light.
Do not shrink, or shiver, shudder or faint.
Walk quietly in.
Embrace the space of knowing that contains all you need.
Hug the peace that surpasses all understanding.
God is I AM.
I AM is there.
Be there, in the Holiest of Holies, present with the
Ever-Present God, I AM, Who is God Alone!!!"

By Inspiration of God the Holy Spirit
via Nawanna Lewis Miler

Psalm 30:11-12 – "Thou hast turned for me my mourning into dancing: thou hast put off my sackcloth, and girded me with gladness; to the end that my glory may sing praise to thee, and not be silent. O Lord my God, I will give thanks unto thee forever."

John 14:6 – "Jesus saith unto him, I am the way, the truth, and the life: no man cometh unto the Father, but by me."

2 Timothy 1:9 – "Who hath saved us, and called us with an holy calling, not according to our works, but according to his own purpose and grace, which was given us in Christ Jesus before the world began..."

Most Holy, Loving, Beneficent, Sovereign God, and Creator of the Universe – both the visible and the invisible: You are the Only True, and Living God – The Triune God – The Three in One God. How we love You Holy God! You are the God of all Grace and Glory Who is Incomparably, Exceeding-Greatness. You are Perfectly Holy in all Divine Attributes of Perfection. You are Absolute Truth, Holiness, Power, Peace, Righteousness, Joy, Wisdom, Knowledge and Divinity without division or diversion. You alone are God.

We worship God. You are Life. You are Source. Everything and everyone else are re-sources. Alone, God makes provisions, according to Your Sovereign Will, Most High. You are the "God-All-By-Myself" God, Who is the Eternal and Everlasting God of all Creation – throughout all ages. We humble ourselves in the power of God the Holy Spirit. Through Jesus Christ, our Lord and Savior, we have the limitless, fully embodied Power of God the Holy Spirit in us.

You are God the Son, Who is Jesus Christ, the Sacrificial Lamb. As Jesus Christ Who hang on the Cross of Calvary, You majestically downloaded all the sin of every person upon of Your Son, throughout every age of the world, for all of time, from the beginning of time to the end. You uploaded Your Blessings for us so we could receive Salvation through Jesus Christ at the appointed time, in time. You opened the door, from the God side, so that we could return to You, Father God through Jesus Christ. You are the Open Door. We walk through You, Jesus, back to fellowship with God the Father Who You are! Jesus is the Way, the Truth, the Life, and the only and All-Sufficient Redeemer. You are God in Three Persons – the Only True and Living God. We adore God.

You are God the Holy Spirit! You are the fully vested and invested, Seminal Power for Rebirth of all believers, and all things pertaining to God's Will. You Birth, Rebirth, and Resurrect people from the dead, according to Your Will. Through the process of Regeneration, You make us new. You "re-gene us" and reconfigure our lives through the Regeneration of Salvation. You remake us in the Supernatural Power of God the Holy Spirit. We welcome You Holy Spirit in every thought, vision, idea, line and musing. Most Splendiferously Holy God, God is God.

You are the Power in us as we think Your Thoughts with You, according to Your Holy Will. You are Jehovah Perazim – The God of the Breakings Through. You are the Limitless, Almighty God Who crashes through all perceived impossibilities and predicaments with a single breath of Peace, Strength, and Knowing. When we believe, we see You as You move on our behalf. Nothing is too hard for our Only Superior God.

Holy God, I thought this book was late, almost 25 years late! Now, I realize that I had to walk through the process of time with You, as You unfolded Your Plan. You processed me through all the tenets pertaining to that time; and drew me into greater knowledge of Your Boundless Dimensions, first. Those details were far too many for my limited human mind to know and absorb, or for my spirit to embrace until now. Your Amazing Grace yet overwhelms me.

I see God. You are God! You are Truth. You are Absolute

Supernatural Reality. God is God. There is no other God. How powerful it is to think the thought that You grant us the authority to reminisce with God – the Ancient of Days. What a joy to reflect with You, Divine Creator. What a privilege that You permit such intimacy with Your creations. You are God. Like Psalm 8 says, who am I that You are mindful of me? Yet, You are!

Holy God of the Morning Mercies, I yet see You. Introspectively, I see You as I search deeply within my soul and spirit to hear Your voice; and see the traces of my Master's footsteps throughout my life. Retrospectively, I see You, as You reveal the panoramic view of the distance from which You brought me. How grateful I am that You managed every microscopic detail of my life, even when I didn't know it. Prospectively, I see You, as You reveal the vision of things yet to be accomplished through You.

You are my All-in-All. Your Holy, Loving Grace is everything to me. I see You from countless perspectives, as You integrate all that You have already finished and manifested into the priceless mosaic called life. I sense Your Love and Power through every breath that You permit me to breathe; and everything You permit me to see, and know – visible and invisible.

I see You, as I smell the Sweet Savor of Your Presence, as well-scented jasmine ever abiding with me. I see You, as You permit me to taste and see Your Goodness in impossible situations. I see You as You make Your Voice audible in the darkness of unknowing, so I know that You are with me. I see God – the God of Jesus Christ. As promised, You never leave us alone.

Thank You Holy God for not telling me the whole story, for I know I would not have made the journey to this place called here and now. Self would have forfeited Your blessings upon my life through the disobedience that fear and intimidation so easily prompt. Instead of You, the enemy would have used me against myself.

You never told me all the details of our journey together, except on a need to know basis. Only in hindsight is that cool. Truth? I wanted to know sooner. I almost gave up. Only the fact that I didn't know how to do anything else but love and trust You, and Your love for me, saved my life for this moment. The result is the Grace of foresight and insight now, which I could only acquire from the "going through" in the narrow way. You are the God of my "breakings through".

God: *"I know. I didn't let you kill the plan, the baby who I created and birthed before the foundation of the world, for an appointed time."*

Me: "Thank You God that You didn't give me an opportunity to decide. I wanted a way out! You led me through The Way, forward. Thank You Most Holy and Righteous God!"

The ironies of life overwhelm me, Lord God. The way that You order our steps is often contrary to that which is rational, according to mere human standards. My soul often wondered along the journey if we - You and I together - could have gotten to my next stop on the road a lot faster. Of course, I know the answer is yes. You are God! But, what would I have missed that made me who I am with the information I now bear from You to minister to others? Your timing is perfect. Now, I know that the feelings of inadequacy that a mother feels to birth and raise a child are the same feelings of inadequacy that the preacher feels to accept the call and birth ministry. Both are callings from You. What human is worthy of either? You are the Ever-Present Messiah King.

Majesty, those feelings of inadequacies never leave for those who are called and chosen to proclaim the gospel; parent a child; or anyone who recognizes that we are created and called to serve You, in whatever capacity that calling assumes. Most High and Holy God, Who is yet right here with us, we ask forgiveness for even daring to think that we have a right to input our will – the things we would rather do than what You called us to do. Please forgive us.

God of Mercy and Grace, You alone know that it takes something different to be a woman than to be a man; something else different to be a wife; and something else different to be a mother; and something even more different to be all of those things and be a preacher. How audacious is Your Power and Grace to choose women like me to be Your servant-preacher. How grateful I am to be an instrument in Your Hands. You are the Righteous and Divine Potter Who keeps the Holy Wheel spinning to perfect us.

Awesome Ruler, I love Your lessons of transcendence. Psalm 139 is so absolutely correct. You bless us to understand the awesomeness of David's experience with You. You have already orchestrated all things and people in our lives for Your glory and our best good. I love our conversations, and even the opportunity to have them.

I understand now. This book could not just be a story of my experiences in childbirth. You designed those experiences to be metaphors for life, for anyone, not just women or preachers. If the book were written too soon, I would have missed the application of the birthing experiences to marriage, parenting, accepting the call to ministry, planting a church, planting ministries, pastoring and visions. I would have missed the need for contemporary application to eternal truth. I would have missed the revelation of the mysteries. You are Jehovah Perazim.

God, my missed conceptions were many. Please guide me through this writing. You are trusted to reveal the words to include, according to Your Divine Will. As You have granted the Christ-Mind unto Your daughters and sons, I ask now that You use that mind to recall the details of life that pertain to this work. Please order my steps back through Your history with us, such that even now the knowing of our history is as fresh as Your Morning Mercies.

Thank You, God, for teaching me that surrender to God for conception and birth must be complete, in order to make conception and delivery possible. To give birth, mothers hang in the balance between life and death, so that which was conceived and nurtured may come to life. You are there. We surrender all, Holy Father! Nothing exceeds Your Knowledge or Abilities.

Holy God, my prayer for this work is like that which is recorded for our example in Revelation 1:3. I pray that whoever reads, hears, understands and shares this book, and the truth that is imparted, is abundantly blessed. I believe that You Alone, Holy Spirit, draw the right people to read what is written, even as You speak, teach and guide my thoughts to prepare the truth.

it; and blessed it." *(God Smiles!)*

God: *"I know your end from your beginning! I wrote it; saved it; and blessed it."*

Me: "I thank You God that You do. That makes things a whole lot easier and better. You alone are God!" (I SMILE TOO!) Please Guide me to do all that You desire me to do through this work. As You say in Revelation 1:3, please bless the people who read these words. May they find strength for the journey and enlightenment for their souls!

In the Name of Jesus Christ - Lord God!
Amen!

Chapter 2
Oh God!
We Missed Conceptions!

Luke 1:31 – "And behold, thou shalt conceive in thy womb, and bring forth a son and shalt call His Name Jesus."

Beloved: I was like Sarah in Genesis 16. I was like Rebekah in Genesis 25:21. I was like Rachel in Genesis 31. I was like Hannah in I Samuel 1 and 2. I was like the wife of Manoah, the mother of Samson, in Judges 13. I was like Elizabeth, the mother of John the Baptist, in Luke 1. I was like Mary Magdalene in John 20. I am like Saint Veronica on the Via Dolorosa. I am each of these women and more. And, I have a story that men cannot tell. It takes a woman. For the sake of this writing, I label these women as "God's Wonder Women". They are my mothers, sisters and friends of long standing who defied all of the odds against them.

Indeed, I believe that God calls preachers of the Gospel who are women, just as God calls men. I am one of them. I believe that there are components to God's will, character and essence that only a woman can reveal. God calls each of us who are Christians to reveal a portion of who God is that

14

only we can reveal. The revelation is a result of our encounters with God, as women; whether we give birth to children or not.

With the power of God the Holy Spirit, God calls women. God causes women to bear Jesus in the world, even through our experiences of barrenness. We, too, are preachers who are pregnant. We too are the Theotokas – the God Bearers. I am grateful to men who know and understand. I celebrate Mother Mary, the young Virgin; Elizabeth; the older woman; and Magdalene, the single woman. Jesus did also.

"Listen", as my beloved mentor and exceptional missionary Mrs. Gladiola McDaniel would always say. My prayer is that the story in this book will bless you. It is more challenging for me to write this book than other books God has assigned to my hands because it's very personal, in so many respects. You see, according to my personality profile, I am an introvert, an INFJ Introvert. Smile! However, I will do anything for the cause of Christ. That also includes sharing the most private part of my life – even if I sound a little whacked through the content.

This book is intended to be instructive for all people, male and female. The story that God leads me to share in these pages is a portion of the story that God wrote about me before the foundation of the world. This story was written before I ever drew my first breath; and it requires a preacher to transmit it – a preacher "who happens to be a lady". I trust that you will see your own story within its lines and practical application, regardless of gender or profession.

True to my behavior pattern of faith, let's just jump right in. There is no time to waste. Stay lively.

I think you will understand this thought. I can't do anything that isn't somehow connected to God and the Word of God. Otherwise, it just doesn't matter or make any sense to me. Therefore, the theme of this writing is the birth motif of the Bible, as it played out in real life – my life and the life of my family.

In the Holy Bible, the birth motif or metaphor (life picture in words), is pervasive. That motif is so very critical to our Christian faith. Yet, with the exception of Mary, the Mother of our Lord Jesus, the women mentioned in the stories above were barren for one reason or the other until God moved in supernatural ways to cause conception and birth, against all odds. Their barrenness was a useful and powerful condition in God's plan.

The Wonder Women show us the amazing power of God to work through us, despite conceived or misconceived notions about our predicaments. God the Holy Spirit reminds us that without the barren condition of these women, their stories and the "Miraculous conceptions" would be less impactful, though nonetheless true. Their birthing narratives are some of the memorable stories in the Holy Bible. Their stories are testimonies that our God specializes in achieving the impossible. For God, what humans describe as impossible is irrelevant or non-existent to God's plan. The impossible things, from our point of view, reveal that nothing is too hard for God.

The birth motif is so significant that God uses the physical reality, spiritual metaphor and imagery of birth to describe God's requirement for Christians that "we must be born again", according to John 3:7. The examples of the Wonder Women that are mentioned in the Bible speak to the challenges of biological conception for some women. I too, experienced the same issue. The difficulty of spiritual birth of visions and the plan God has for us is comparable. As a metaphor, the birth motif also speaks to us of the spiritual difficulty of conception and birth that often occurs pertaining to God's call upon our lives. After we read each of the scripture passages pertaining to each of the women, we should stop and think for a minute about what God births or desires to birth, through us, female or male.

If God is perfect, and God is, then God's eternal plan is perfect. God's perfect plan is revealed through the Word of God which is necessary for and applicable to our daily lives. God's perfect plan is revealed to people through revelations, dreams and visions, as well. Let's be clear. God never aborts God's perfect plan. Case closed. Even if we have the difficulty of conception and delivery, either physically or spiritually, God's Word has the power within itself to get "itself" (the plan) done. The Word and all people, places, and things pertaining to it never returns void, according to Isaiah 55:11. If God said it, it is so. Done!

Even those of us who are Post-Resurrection Christians are often challenged to understand, trust, or believe what God does, all of the time. No doubt, some of the Wonder Women missed the conception of their first child, during all the years that they waited, through many years of disappointments. Yet, God worked through the women because God's perfect plan included works that God would move through their offspring. The long delay was not God's denial, even though it seemed impossible to conceive. Clearly, the unlimited power of God's supernatural intervention made conception possible.

With the Biblical frames of reference to birth, parallels may be drawn between them and our own experiences to work with God to bring to pass the visions and assignments God gives us. The parallel is drawn between the impossible situation of which humankind speaks, and the reality of faith that God requires us to possess to accomplish God's perfect will. God permitted the "Wonder Women" to overcome the obstacles to faith to give birth to what God ordained, no matter how difficult the situation was or appeared to be. "Pala!" Is anything too hard for God? Nothing is too hard for God.

For a few pages, please let me just bring you up to speed on two of the characters in this contemporary story pertaining to the birth motif. It is a story of faith in God's perfect plan.

When I arrived as a student in the eighth grade at H.M. Turner High School in Atlanta, Georgia in 1964, he was already there in the 10th grade – a sophomore. His homeroom class was diagonally across the hall from mine. The first time I caught a glimpse of him, he wore a burgundy, long sleeved, V-necked, sweater over a crisply starched white shirt, and dark dress trousers. I didn't know it then, but God was up to the performance of God's plan. Our proximity to each other was our Boaz and Ruth setup. I was not looking for a boyfriend, though. I later found out that he was a practicing Christian, smart, sophisticated, well-dressed, and well-bred. BUT, he was a street dude.

We remained in those homeroom classes until graduation. He was two years older than me. I saw him, but he never saw me. The description sounds like a contradiction. It was. For three years, we passed each other in the hall. But, I was only interested in my books.

In the fall of 1967, he was among the first African American students who integrated Georgia State (University) in downtown Atlanta. Back then, there was an after school ritual or practice for high school students in Atlanta that those who participated in it will never forget. There were only five high schools for us in the city. The socially cool and aggressively pursued ritual for high school students was to gather under the clock of the Rich's Department Store on Broad Street, after school. We mostly people-watched, I would say; but some transferred buses to go home or work.

This was a new beginning for us as African Americans. Civil Rights and access to college broadened in ways that were never realized before. The older college students from Emory University, Georgia State College (University) and Georgia Tech (College) gathered "on the yard" at the Atlanta

University Center (AUC). The AUC included Morehouse College; Clark College; Spelman College; and Morris Brown College. To cruise the vicinity, on gas that was less than one per ($1.00) gallon, was a big deal. Credit did not exist for us.

On the basement escalator of that Rich's Department Store, in the heart of downtown Atlanta, God brought me to my future husband, like God brought Eve to Adam. I didn't know that then. George C. Miller, Jr. was riding down the escalator on the left side. I was riding up on the right side. He yelled across the escalators as we passed each other, for me to wait for him at the top. I thought that was rather rude; however, he came back up to the escalator.

To me, George and I really did not seem like a good match. Yet, in some mysterious way, the match seemed right; except it did not make sense. After a month of visiting me at our home, he asked me if he "could have a chance", as MALES used to ask, not females. I really was concerned about how my parents, especially my Dad, would feel about me dating a college student who was two years older than I. That factor brought about a bit of Daddy's stern looks and harsh comments which were designed to protect me. But, that was not the biggest issue.

The bigger issue was that we were totally and completely the opposite of each other. We had few things in common, except our Christian faith, intellect, similar upbringing, love of people, and the ability to dance. One of us was left-brained. The other was right-brained. I can't remember which was which, at the time, anymore. He was and is an extrovert. I was and am yet an introvert. His friends were totally different from mine, although all friends became mutual treasures to this day. He was one of the "Arrogant Nine" who started the first chapter of Omega Psi Phi Fraternity on a predominantly white campus in the Deep South. The brothers of Zeta Theta Chapter were smart, courageous and strong. George was very different from me.

So, I talked to God about the relationship before I agreed that we should date, especially since I was not looking for a boyfriend. This seemed like it just might be God's plan in action, except... you guessed it... I didn't know it then. I thank God that both of us were active in the church! I said, "God, we don't seem to match. But if this is the person that You choose for me, then teach me how to love him." On September 18, 1967, we started "going together".

I am quite sure, in retrospect, that God the Holy Spirit prompted that prayer. Every Sunday, we were in either Bethlehem Baptist Church, his family's church, or Flipper Temple A.M.E. Church, my family's church. Both of us grew up and actively participated in our respective churches. Later, we added a couple of churches to visit. I prayed at both. We dated for five years before we were married.

I often tell the story of the day I really learned the meaning of faith and how to wait on the Lord. It was the day I learned to wait on George Miller. After graduation from college, God blessed George with a very good position in the Commercial Lending Management Training Program at Trust Company Bank (now SunTrust).

Hiring minorities was still a new phenomenon in corporate America, and banks in particular. There were four or five men who were the first African Americans in the Bank's Management Training Program. That was huge, though we didn't really have a full grasp of its significance at the time. George and I were scheduled to attend a major formal dinner function for the Bank that related to the Atlanta business community. To be at the dinner was important to George's career, as well.

While on summer break from the University of Georgia, I worked as a researcher to compile an African American Annotated Bibliography for Carnegie-Atlanta Public Library. We were hired as students to do the preliminary work for what became The Auburn Avenue Research Library on African American Culture. I got off work at 12 Noon that day because the library closed early on Saturdays.

George was scheduled to pick me up there, as usual, but he was late. I was obnoxiously compulsive about punctuality back then, and now. That pretty much drove him nuts because he never understood "the rush" or the need to be on time. I waited patiently on the steps of the Library, as all the employees exited. As divinely ordered, no one offered me a ride or help. God primed me for lessons in faith.

He said he would be there. He always picked me up, even if he was late. I waited through various scenarios that played out in my head. In front of my face, an assortment of characters drifted pass. I didn't leave to catch the bus because I thought I would miss him; and there was no such thing as a cell phone. I waited for seven straight hours, on the concrete steps, in downtown Atlanta, in July. He finally arrived at 7:00 P.M. George said he would be there. I believed him. The dinner started a few blocks away.

The conversation that followed really doesn't matter. The fact that we missed this important event no longer matters, though it did then. What matters most is that in my waiting, God taught me an incredible lesson and gave me a remarkable fruit that would influence the rest of my life. Something so simple became monumental to my faith. That was the moment, the all-encompassing, all-important moment that I learned to wait on the Lord, for all things.

George and I married when he was 23 and I was 21. Our wedding day was August 13, 1972, a month before the start of my senior year at the University of Georgia. It was also approximately the same time that God intersected our paths on the escalator at Rich's, five years earlier. We dated for five years, from the time I was 16 and he was an 18 years-old college freshman. While dating, George earned his B.B.A. Degree, and subsequently the M.B.A. I finished UGA at the end of the Fall Semester in 1972, four months after we married. I took a double load most semesters to finish in three and a half years.

When I reflect on those years at UGA, I remember that every Friday at noon, I travelled home on the Greyhound Bus, the 65 miles from Athens to Atlanta. Every Sunday night, George drove me through the dark backwoods to Athens, Georgia in his blue, 1961 Ford Falcon that had no heat. Wrapped in blankets during the winter months, we did that routine for 3.5 years. Often one of his Omega Psi Phi Fraternity brothers or friends rode along to keep him company on the way back, late at night. And every week, before the two-hour trip back to Athens, George and I would clean up Chesterfield Finance Company, one of his part-time jobs. We cleaned together. We climbed together.

From my earliest childhood, I always thought and really believed I would have 12 children. I believed I would get married and my husband and I would have 12 children. Point blank. There was no doubt in my mind, though George questioned the number 12. I believed God told me that.

During the dating process, we talked about our future children often. When others asked, through the years, why he married me, my husband gave one answer, with a two-pronged response, consistently. He said and would probably yet say, "I married her because of her mind. She was very smart and I thought she would be a great mother for our children." In other words, the fact that I was a cute, petite, 98 pounds, intelligent, well-put together young lady had nothing to do with the choice, right? Smile! I just had to throw that in there.

For the first seven years of our marriage, we missed conception of a baby. Five of those years, we lived in our native city of Atlanta, Georgia. Time after time, these wonderful, well-credentialed doctors told me we would never have children. One after the other, for five years, the same report was given. I could not hear them because that was "not what God told me" is what kept playing in my heart and my head. Besides, we planned to be parents.

In 1976, Former Governor of Georgia Jimmy Carter was elected President of the United States. George worked in his campaign, and on the Transition Team. We attended all of the celebrations for President Carter, including the victory party at the Georgia World Congress Center. On January 20, 1977, we attended our first Presidential Inauguration, ever, together. God blessed us so tremendously, on so many levels.

I too was blessed to work in the Communications Department of the Atlanta Chamber of Commerce with some incredible people. Tom Hamill was the Executive Director; my outstanding boss was Robert Brennan, former News Director at a local television station; and photographer Dennis Yaschik was amazing with the lens. I am just now realizing that George and I were so young to be exposed to such phenomenal people and opportunities. We participated in so many great events and moments. God granted us access to such powerful decision makers in the business, religious, social, political and financial arenas. The blessings of grace flowed over us, even in our early twenties.

As a result of their volunteer work with the Transition Team, George and Joe Norton were asked to drive President-Elect Jimmy Carter's Transition Papers to Washington, D.C. That request was a really big, secretive deal that we really didn't completely comprehend, at the time. You understand that this was way before technology raised up. There was no

Google, map quests, travel drives, or cell phones. All of the President-Elects collective information to begin his Administration was on that truck. We were more than a little nervous, but not fully aware of the politics of all that. Our naiveté adds a whole new meaning to the phrase ignorance is bliss. Now, we know to be responsible to deliver all the documents and plans of the President-Elect of the United States was a special honor and privilege,.

The Bank gave George an extended leave of absence to work on the Transition Team in Washington, D.C. He subsequently became a political appointee in the Carter Administration in the Office of the Secretary of Treasury. Against my will, but clearly in the will of God, I quit my job at the Atlanta Chamber of Commerce, and we moved to Washington. With so many wonderful blessings swirling around us, it was difficult to get our heads and hearts in sync to realize that we were tied up in a spiritual, physical, and emotional situation about which we could do nothing. In my head, it just was not possible to embrace the negative report that we would never be parents according to several of the best doctors in Obstetrics and Gynecology.

We didn't want to talk about having children to our greatly loved, well-intentioned family and friends. Many determined in their minds that it was way past time for us to have a baby. We didn't want to talk about it to each other either, if the truth is told. Though not spoken, each of us was concerned that we would say the wrong thing. We had all we needed to bring a child into the world. But, we had a real problem that only God could solve.

The repetitive diagnosis was that I had a number of uterine fibroid tumors. A common diagnosis now, we knew my diagnosis for years, when the condition got worse. Our parenting plan's potential grew dim. The time had come to consider adoption, according to George. Adoption is indeed a marvelous, loving course of action for parenting. I was not opposed to adoption, though I did not believe it was God's final action for us. My mind and heart remained open.

While looking for employment in Washington, my days often ended in Lafayette Park across the street from the White House. Woefully unprepared for that to which I was introduced, I met and engaged in extensive listening sessions with the homeless people. To me, they too were God's people who deserved my kindness. Ministry to them, was always a part of me after that, even now. Eventually, I worked two part time jobs as an editor, and began work on my Masters in Organizational Communications at Howard University's Graduate School of Arts and Sciences.

One evening, I watched the national news at home, alone. A story came on that really grabbed my attention. No. The word "grabbed" really doesn't even begin to describe how I was stopped in my tracks, without any knowledge whatsoever of what was to come next. The news showed a physician who testified as an expert before the U.S. Congress. He was an OB/GYN who was also the head of Fetal Internal Medicine at George Washington University Hospital, a well-known teaching hospital in Washington, where he was also a professor.

Why was I so immediately engrossed in the new findings pertaining to fetal alcohol syndrome? God arrested my attention. I didn't drink and the reports said I would never be pregnant. So, why was I so totally enamored with this doctor and his research? I told George about him when he came home later, and could hardly wait till morning to call that doctor, as God led me to do. His name was Dr. Sergio Fabro. God's plan was manifesting. I didn't know that then.

His number was easy enough to find because he was also the Director of Obstetrics and Gynecology at Columbia Hospital for Women in Washington. His credentials were through the roof, I learned later. The very next morning, first thing, I dialed the number. A man with a wispy, whimsical, strong yet light-hearted, joyful and heavily accented voice answered the phone. It was he, the man himself, who I heard testify before the U.S. Congress the day before. He answered his own phone. Unbelievable! I prayed. The providence of God was at work.

The conversation proceeded like I was talking to an old friend that I had not seen for a while, and had to bring him up to date. He was very familiar to me, yet we had never met. At first, he compassionately and yet regretfully informed me that there was no way possible that he could add me to his patients. Though he was incredibly kind and emphatically precise when he told me that he was not taking any new patients, God nudged me to tell Him how he may be our last hope to have a baby. I did as God directed me.

Even now, 37 years later, thankful tears form in my spirit and eyes, as I write this portion. Dr. Fabro was clearly extremely well-learned; much sought-after as a physician; and without a doubt well over-extended. I am sure that I must have sounded like thousands of other women in the same predicament. Nevertheless, Dr. Fabro changed his mind; and gave me an appointment date. That was unbelievable. Transplanted people who were from other places were not that kind in the nation's capital, even though the native Washingtonians were. We would not dare miss the appointment, which we learned was made through a big exception to the rule. God was up to something. I could not take another missed conception, for they were many! God overwhelmed me, and we had to respond to the movement of God. We had to be present for the designated time.

When we arrived, as divinely appointed, we immediately encountered the magnificent Dr. Fabro. He was unreal - so full of life. I just knew he was the right doctor for me. Everything about him said a resounding yes. This time he was chatting with his Administrative Assistant when we entered. She was a young, vibrant, delightful woman who would become a precious jewel to us, and fast friend to me. The man's presence just filled up the office and the exam room, everywhere that he was. Observing him was like watching a medical machine in action. Yet, he had the greatest, genuine concern ever as his bedside manner.

Following the exam, George and I sat to listen to Dr. Fabro's findings. He apologized that his results were as other doctors said. He began to read off the sizes of the tumors that sounded like a grocery list for the produce section of a supermarket. He said that the "big one – the big H" (hysterectomy) - would have to be done very soon. However, what he said next changed our lives, forever.

With that wonderful, endearing, profound, Italian-sounding accent, he said, "If you want to have baby, we have baby right away. But we must hurry. There is a dangerous situation going on here." For over 15 years, since my teen years, Dr. Fabro's voice was the first and only human, voice of hope that believed I could birth a baby. He said, "We must hurry and have a baby". We were elated with the report. This genius believed birth of our baby was possible, despite the odds. So did George and Nawanna.

A few weeks later, I went to see Dr. Fabro because I was really sick. I thought the fibroids were kicking up. They were. They were growing with good reason, though dangerously so. I was pregnant. God worked on our behalf, in spite of the impediments, just for us, or so it seemed. When I learned the news, I drove the few blocks from Columbia Hospital for Women down Pennsylvania Avenue, circled the block, around the Treasury Building, and turned right onto East Executive Avenue. At the time, that street ran between the U.S. Treasury Building and the White House, but was closed off after 911. I pulled in front of the second floor window to George's office and began to honk the horn. He looked out. Security started to walk toward me, so I yelled, "WE ARE HAVING A BABY", before I knew it.

The guards who George talked to daily started to cheer, and were almost as happy as we were. They were very proud of William Beckham, who was an Assistant Secretary, Azie Taylor Morton, who was the first African American Treasurer of the United States, and George in their uncommon appointments in the Carter Administration. People waiting in line to enter the White House across the street cheered, as well. That was a real, dramatic, made-for-television moment. Except, George couldn't believe what he thought he heard. He motioned that he was coming down to me. I circled the block, again. He got in the car and I told him the whole episode of our story that he missed. "We are having a baby", he said in quiet resolve. He was stunned, speechless, overwhelmed, elated, but reserved.

On a subsequent visit to Dr. Fabro's office, the ultrasound showed the little baby nestled among fibroid tumors that were growing. Yikes! I was forewarned that would happen at the first doctor's visit. It was coming to pass. The tumors were growing rapidly in size right along with the baby. The same nourishment from the prenatal vitamins that the baby received, the fibroids received, also. Horrible was and is yet the thought. At the rate the tumors were growing, the probability that they would cause a miscarriage was extremely high. We were in the midst of a high risk pregnancy.

Despite all the warnings, I continued the Master's program, though I had to give up one of the part time jobs. I took one minute at a time. However, at the start of the spring semester and the second trimester, things got a bit tricky. Serious threats of miscarriage presented. The pain was excruciating. Nevertheless, Dr. Fabro only spoke power and good thoughts, never fear. He knew the dangers from the statistics that he shared, but we were his project; and he was as determined as we were to bring our baby into the world. He was as fully invested as we were. We were on one accord about the reality of a baby being born into the world.

Threats of premature birth or worse kept George and me going to the hospital, frequently. For the next four months, Dr. Fabro placed me on complete bedrest and a magnum of red wine to be consumed every day to manage the very strong contractions. The doctor closely monitored me with telephone calls and the more than usual visits to his office. George worked extremely long hours in the President's Administration, but he was present with me.

So, at night my husband froze the magnum of red wine. In the morning, he would bring it upstairs, and set it beside the bed before he went to work. Our friends were great, but few. Dora and Charlie Baker, and Loretta and Willie Cadwell were God-sent. I would muster up enough energy to make dinner for George; but, for the most part, my life and our baby's life were tied to faith, prayer, and red wine. Now that I really reflect on those days, I marvel at the fact that God chose the noted expert in fetal alcohol syndrome research as my doctor. His prescription for me was red wine. Yet, prior to this experience or afterwards, I did not drink; but was never intoxicated from the prescription.

On May 17, 1979, George and I attended the 25th Anniversary Commemoration of Brown V. Board of Education at the White House. In his opening remarks, President Jimmy Carter gave honor to the great pioneer, A. Philipp Randolph, who died the night before, May 16, 1979, one day after my 28th birthday. As you know, A. Philipp Randolph founded the Brotherhood of Sleeping Car Porters, and was one of the early leaders of the Civil Rights Movement that I vividly remember. I always admired him. So, his passing made me sad. He is yet said to be the mastermind behind the 1963 March on Washington, along with his protégé Bayard Rustin. I wrote a research paper in college on both men and their phenomenal work..

Immediately after President Carter finished his speech, George took me to a sitting area outside of the Green Room. He split his time between me and the reception. Momentarily, one of the Assistants brought another great man who I admired, as much as I admired A. Phillip Randolph, since early childhood, to sit next to me. It was the stalwart of education, Dr. Benjamin E. Mays, President Emeritus of Morehouse College in Atlanta. I was stunned as my thoughts were collected. God orchestrated a divine appointment and intersection that is yet difficult to adequately articulate even now. It was an unbelievable moment – the God moment.

When I was a child, I often walked the long way home from Church, especially during Vacation Bible School and choir rehearsal in the summer. That longer way, which really was out of my way, took me pass the campus of Morehouse College. Often, I saw Dr. Mays walk across its hallowed landscape with such authority, strength, and elegance, along with his students. He was a tall, imposing, and distinguished figure, who seemed almost synonymous with Morehouse.

That illustrious institution, since its founding, produced and yet produces, some great, phenomenal, African American men who are/were fathers, educators, clergy, teachers, doctors, lawyers, judges, statesmen, researchers, leaders... The graduates impacted, and yet impact, the world, like the Rev. Dr. Martin Luther King, Jr. God would later teach me about divine appointments; and Dr. Mays is yet identified as a Mystic. Morehouse selects the men.

The thought grabbed me that George and I stood in long lines at the viewing to pay our respects to Dr. King at Morehouse the day before the funeral. By nothing but the Grace of God, George, my sister Collette, her future husband Ronald, and I walked just a few rows behind the cortege after Dr. King's funeral on April 9, 1968, except we were not noted dignitaries. We walked all the way from Ebenezer Baptist Church to the campus of Morehouse College for his temporary interment. We did that for Dr. King. We did it for ourselves. We did it for our children whose birth was yet questionable, at best.

Dr. Mays was very feeble at the Commemoration Celebration, but he made the journey to the moment – the celebration of history – by train or car. I can't remember. He didn't fly on planes. For me, that time was our God-ordained moment! Both of us were present, and there was a child in our midst whose birth and life were yet uncertain. Neither this great pioneer nor I would miss this historic event that meant so much to our people and us. At the time, Dr. Mays was far more fully vested in the contributions he made to the world, and the education of African Americans than I. I was yet a dreamer, who was greatly blessed and honored to be in the presence of this great man.

I shared with Dr. Mays my admiration and respect for him, through the years. Of course, he knew of the terrain across which I traversed in Atlanta, including Fair Street bottom, where Morehouse is yet located. He knew about the top of the hill, on Fair Street, where I worshipped at Flipper Temple A.M.E. Church, just up the street from Morehouse. Though I met him before, I would not dare to insult the genius of the man to recall the occasions. Talking to Dr. Mays, in that moment, was like talking directly to the Mystic that he was known to be or an angel – God's prophetic messenger. God is so absolutely amazing.

He very kindly asked me about the delivery date that was, without a doubt, very obviously imminent. I just said, "The baby is two weeks late, we think. That is the other reason why I am here. My husband did not want to leave me at home alone, 30 miles away."

What I wanted to say, but did not say, was that the same vitamins and nutrients that caused the baby to grow healthily were causing the tumors to grow simultaneously. I wanted to say that even in normal circumstances the same nutrients could cause the baby to begin to calcify, if delivery is delayed too long. I wanted to say that Dr. Fabro's hesitation was that one or more of the fibroids could be cut in the process of the Caesarian. I could bleed to death and the baby could suffocate in my blood. I couldn't tell him any of that. There was no way that I would burden this distinguished gentleman with my issues. We were there to celebrate the historic milestone. We were blessed.

Dr. Mays just smiled that incredibly quiet, kind smile, and said, "If it is a male child send 'them' to Morehouse." I affirmed his instructions with an emphatic, but humbled, "Yes Sir!" It was years before I realized that this Christian Mystic, this man of God, this man who yet had a powerful command of the English language despite his years, used a plural pronoun instead of a singular one. God's messenger spoke his generational blessing over our sons. It was enough. I was encouraged. It was indeed a Godly moment that made me stronger for the journey ahead.

In some strange way, May 17, 1979, is a marker for me now. That date was not just the 25th anniversary of the great decision of Brown V. Board of Education that makes it important for me, though that alone is glorious. God pinpointed that date in my life for me, as a date that I would need to remember, in days and years ahead. God is God. God handles our details, if we permit.

After driving 60 miles round trip three days a week for eight months and pregnant for nine months plus, the first year of the Master's program was completed. I am yet filled with gratitude for what God did on our behalf. It is amazing how much God does for us without our full understanding of the challenges. God walks us through the land mines without our knowledge. Every Sunday, we were in Church. Yet, in many ways, we were alone. Our immediate family was all in Atlanta. We knew people in the Carter Administration, and three other couples, but that was essentially it. We had plenty of company to visit us from out of town. However, no one knew the full gravity of the situation, except my husband, Dr. Fabro, and me. We just asked people to pray for us.

Dr. Fabro was the only doctor who ever said anything close to a word of hope about having a baby. Others looked at the raggedy state of the womb and declared birth was impossible. Dr. Fabro looked at the impossible and said what we desired would happen anyway. He was wired to God. He was the one we needed. He was the one God chose through whom God would work the Miracle. I wonder how much better off we would be if we would just wait on the Lord? For God's grace to us, my mind is adrift into an old gospel song of my youth, in silent tears! "He is so good to me. Oh, Yes. He gives me victory. Oh, yes. Oh, what a mighty God we serve." I still sing that from time to time.

Musings with God the Holy Spirit!

- We never know what the next move of God is.

- Live in expectant hope and anticipation.
- We must learn to trust the arrangements that God already made for absolutely everything God ordains.
- For every action there is a corresponding re-action.
- Failure to respond when God prompts us is disobedience that will delay our blessings.
- We must routinely, deliberately and systematically listen for the Voice of God, at all times.
- Most of the time, God speaks through unconventional means, which validate the fact that God speaks.
- God is not limited to our methods of human existence.
- No report that humans give is final, but rather an indication for future testimony about the amazing power of God.
- We always believe the report of the Lord in God's Word and Divine REVELATION.
- Always, expect the unexpected.
- The unexpected does not catch God by surprise.
- God's provisions are already made for the expected and the unexpected.
- We do not know how nor when, we just believe God can (trust) and God will (faith).
- Contrary to popular belief, God does NOT make a way. The way was already made before the beginning of time or the foundation of the world.
- Jesus is THE WAY, THE TRUTH, THE LIFE!

Chapter 3
Oh God!
You Alone Decide!

Mark 8:23-25 – "And he took the blind man by the hand, and led him out of the town; and when he had spit on his eyes, and put his hands upon him he asked him if he saw anything. And he looked up, and said, I see men as trees, walking. After that he put his hands again upon his eyes, and made him look up: and he was restored, and saw every man clearly."

For the next eight days, I was in excruciating pain when we went to see Dr. Fabro for the final weekly appointment. We knew that one way or the other, something had to happen that week. During the end of the last month of the third trimester, the appointments are generally weekly. My weekly actually became almost daily. I was in labor - hard, serious labor - that produced no results for weeks. Thoroughly exhausted doesn't even begin to describe my condition. I was freeze-framed in pain. On the last visit, Dr. Fabro's constant pep talks and ever-optimistic conversations turned terribly somber, as they did during the process when he had to tell us something medical that was not so good.

He said that essentially the tumors were everywhere. He reminded me about the possibility of a rupture of one or more of them during delivery, and that possibility I could bleed to death. He reminded me that a Cesarean was not really an option on the front end – only in an emergency. Very pedantically, he explained again. If he did a Cesarean, one or more of the tumors could be cut; and I could bleed to death. So, the decision was made to wait the process out to the very last moment. Once again, he repeated the question that I hated most. This was the final warning and the final answer. He spoke with the voice of a loving father, teacher, doctor, friend, and a fellow traveler on this journey with us. Those descriptions have to run altogether like that because he was all of that – a gift from God to us.

With his calm, though somewhat grave, more heavily accented than usual voice, the exact opposite of the man I first encountered that day in his office, Dr. Fabro said, "What is amazing is that we are here. It is a Miracle from God. Things could get a lot more difficult now. That is why I have to ask you the question again." He stopped talking and looked at my husband who was obviously overwhelmed. The silence was obtrusive and poignant. I knew what was coming. I waited, as my answer was framed.

Then he continued, "If it comes down to a choice of who should be saved, do you choose to save the baby or yourself?" Confidently and conclusively, I said, "Thank you, again, Dr. Fabro. Again, I tell you that we can't make that decision. If it comes down to that, God will decide."

That was it. Hugs were given all around. In my spirit, the team was ready – God; the incredible doctor; my magnificent husband/father; a little baby; and I. That's how I saw it. Dr. Fabro totally understood me. That's all. I totally understood Dr. Fabro. George and I were on one accord, in faith. My responsibility was to take the decision off my husband's shoulders, should things go wrong.

And so, the date was May 25, 1979, twelve years after George and I started dating and seven years after we married when everything would be decided. We arrived at George Washington University Hospital at approximately 7:00 a.m. Labor was in fact in full swing for several days, but the delivery was not close. The baby was breached and the contractions were insufficient to deliver. So, we were instructed to walk.

We walked, very, very slowly for 12 hours with periodic check-ins with the nurse and Dr. Fabro. Eight days after I made the affirmation with Dr. Mays, the male child was born around 11:00 p.m. I profusely, but quietly thanked God for our son, George III, who persisted to arrive healthy and beautiful at almost nine pounds. We brought him home to Fairfax, Virginia, and the new home we purchased a few months prior. My Mother arrived from Atlanta. She was my angel in my room. We were extremely grateful to God.

However, our elation and exuberance were put on hold the day after we went home from the hospital. Thank God, my Mother was there to take care of the baby and me because something went terribly wrong. Once more, I knew the enemy was attempting to take me out. I knew I was dying. My husband carried me to the car for the journey back to the hospital and Dr. Fabro. God's Spirit was felt as I lay in the back seat. God took control. As we drove the 30 miles distance back from Fairfax to Washington, D.C., it was pretty easy for George and me to know that I was in very big trouble. The familiar scenery through the I-95 corridor, across the Potomac River, became one big blur. God helped me to focus my mind on one itsy-bitsy image at a time; and hold that image until I could grasp another.

Spiritually and emotionally, the feeling was like swinging from one rope to another, ever mindful not to drop off. When I would start to drift into unconsciousness, God interrupted me; and I could hear the sound of my husband's voice calling me, though it seemed very far away. George wrapped me in a blanket, in May, because I had massive chills, sort of like iceberg level chills, that took up residence in my body. I began to shake profusely with consciousness being snipped away. I didn't want my husband to see that. God took me into the zone. God the Holy Spirit said, "Think with me." With the Spirit, I thought, "If I lose consciousness that will be it. I will not lose consciousness. Hold on to your consciousness. Stay", I said repeatedly to myself. "Stay, Nawanna!"

God helped me to think in prayer. "God please help me to stop shaking. If I frighten George, we could end up in the Potomac River and that will be it. We have a new baby. One of us has to be here. I prefer both of us. God, I really don't want George to be afraid. God please take control. If I make him afraid that will make me upset. If I get upset, that will make things worse." God helped me to remain calm and so every time George asked me how was I or was I okay, God helped me to respond affirmatively. "Yes!"

For seven days, I was in the hospital with a life-threatening staph infection that I received from there. The doctors and the nurses were really alarmed. The transfusions seemed endless! I have really small veins that roll. The transfusions really horrified me. The very idea of placing someone else's blood in my veins had me going crazy. There were warnings about contracting Hepatitis. The doctors, nurses and techs assured me I had no other choice. God talked me into a place of gratitude and submission. Reluctantly, the papers were signed. Surely, God would not permit us to go through all of this to be infected with bad blood. "Amazing Grace, how sweet the sound…"

For seven days, George and my Mother brought the baby to see me in the hospital. And, for seven days, they went home without me, which was emotionally wrenching. Early in the morning, on the eighth day, I decided with God that I was going home. The constant reminder from some of the nurses that if I left the hospital I could die were overthrown. Dr. Fabro agreed with me that I should go home. Through the birth of our firstborn son, God taught me some incredible lessons of the Spirit, and changed our lives forever. The "no" of humans is not God's "no"! Prayer is critical to maintain faith in God in the midst of adversity. It is not just cliché, but Biblical. God does indeed take the foolish things of this world to confound the wise. Nothing is too hard for God. Heaven and hell are real.

From the second hospitalization, in a real way, God taught me the Theology that sometimes we need a second touch from the Lord to complete the process of healing like the blind man who Jesus healed. Don't despair or complain when you think you have been delivered from something, only to experience what looks like a setback in your deliverance and healing. We may experience the enemy's attempt at sabotage; or maybe the process has two steps. Sometimes, we are forced to look UP for a different view, so that we can see straight or right.

Either way, Jesus never does a botched job on us or leaves anything incomplete pertaining to us. Trust God. What Jesus does is always phenomenal. All the things I looked forward to doing for so long during the first week of our first baby's life, I missed. Thank God, my Mother was there who had managed care for a great number of newborn babies. I missed his first feeding because Mama added rice cereal to his diet, immediately. She said he was big and hungry. I was blessed to watch his first bath in his little tub, at home, after the umbilical cord dropped off.

My Mother was overly meticulous about the baby's care which made me completely at ease. That too spoke to my soul that God is intricately concerned about us. As the Bible records, God is aware of every hair that falls from our head and drops to the ground. God is also aware of every umbilical cord that is cut; and the remaining cord when it dries up and falls off.

My Mother was a fountain of love, faith, knowledge and peace. She cooked George three lavish meals a day; and provided the best care possible for the baby and me. Mama and George took him to his first visit with the pediatrician for whom we searched long and extensively. His name is Dr. Kermit Simrel, who opened his practice in Washington a short time before our son became one of his first patients. Like God led me to Dr. Fabro, God led us to Dr. Simrel. He was well credentialed and practiced medicine with some old, traditional folkways he learned from helping to care for a host of siblings. Needless to say, my Mother greatly approved. The Director of Children's Hospital highly recommended him to George at a social event they attended. Indeed, Dr. Simrel was the best doctor for us!

In the days and months ahead, I learned to sing every line of every verse of many hymns in the hymnbook that I didn't already know to a child who never slept. This mother needed those hymns, too, because I very rarely slept either because the baby was awake. My care of our baby boy was most deliberate and intentional in every way, as I saw my Mother's example. Hymns are still my absolute favorite music. We are reminded that nothing is ever wasted when we put all things in the hands of God. God reveals how they work for God's glory and our good. Patient trust in God will carry us to a place in God that nothing else will. Waiting on the Lord is paramount to accomplish everything. Don't get ahead of God. Romans 8:28 is always true, as is the entirety of the Bible. There is always a compelling urge to follow God's lead.

Musings with God the Holy Spirit!

- Females are born with all the eggs they will ever have nestled in the womb.
- Eggs represent the potential of what can be birthed.
- Spiritually, through God the Holy Spirit, we, male and female, are born again with all we need within us to achieve God's plan.
- If Jeremiah 1:5 is true and it is, then God the Holy Spirit births us in the earth with specific, encoded details to who we are called to be.
- Neither the condition of the womb nor the individual components for birth prevent the implementation of God's plan.
- Therefore, the individual elements of that which is to be birthed in the earth are not prevented.
- Just as a female is born with all the eggs she will ever have, the eggs represent the potential of the vision for all good things that God already placed in us; and the plan God already made for us.
- The eggs represent the potential within us to realize every vision and dream that God gives us.
- We have to create an atmosphere in real time for the reproduction of the dreams and visions God gives us, despite the conditions or circumstances.
- We must stand firm in faith and waiver not

Chapter 4
Oh God!
The Gestation is Scary!

Jeremiah 17:7-8 - "But blessed is the one who trusts in the Lord, whose confidence is in Him. They will be like a tree planted by the water that sends out its root by the stream. It does not fear when heat comes; its leaves are always green. It has no worries in a year of drought and never fails to bear fruit."

In the fall, after our first son, George C. Miller, III, was born, I returned to the Master's Program at Howard. In my head, I thought it was most necessary, lest I lose momentum, never to recover it. So, I cared for the baby all day. I studied when he slept which was almost never. I went to classes at night; and slept three hours each night. When I woke up for the 3:00 a.m. feeding, I didn't go back to sleep. That forever changed my sleep pattern. I would not complain; and there was no help. Really, God helped me through the hymns I sang, relentlessly. George worked 12 to 16-hour days in the Carter Administration. "Do what you must do to get it done", I said, over and over.

One Saturday in early September, I packed our new baby boy in the car to go pick up the sitter. My plan was to get way ahead in the research and writing. George traveled a great deal; and I had to get the study in whenever possible. Though I would be home, I needed Cynthia to watch the baby, while I compiled the research and wrote the papers.

As we drove back home, and I approached a traffic light that was turning red, I slowed to accommodate the distance to the intersection. Before I came to a complete stop, I heard the Lord say, "Stop right there. Do not go any further." I did as I was told. Then I heard, "Look". As instructed, I looked quickly in the rearview mirror; and saw a car speeding toward me as I sat still. Thoughts were racing through my mind, probably faster than she was driving.

"She is going to hit me. Oh no! Stop! My baby!" I prayed that one word prayer – "JESUS". All I could do was jam my foot with all my might on the brake, but I could not prevent the collision. WHAM! Just like that, my knee was forced into the steering column and my head was slammed into the stirring wheel, though my seatbelt was fastened. All I could think about was getting to my baby. I was getting out of that car, as fast as greased lightning, despite onlookers who told me to do otherwise. My baby was in the back seat. He didn't cry. "My baby! Oh my God! Please! Help us."

Help us, God did. The baby was knocked up out of the car seat and perched against the side of it, in the rear in an awkward position. The seat belt protected him, but he didn't cry, a fact that frightened me for a moment. Suddenly, we were unwilling participants in the midst of an unscheduled crash test or something. It turned out that the baby was really just asleep and basically undisturbed by the whole incident. Yes! That too was God. He never slept.

When I went to see the person behind us and the car that hit us, a young woman was there. She cried and spoke hysterically. She said something about how sorry she was, and how bad things were in her life... that she had just broke up with her boyfriend. She was very distraught, but sustained no obvious injuries. So I hugged her and left her with bystanders. No doubt, the condition of her car and the wreck itself sent her off to a bad place. Plus, it was quite obvious that her car was totaled. The evidence was clear that none of us should have walked away from that accident.

How humbly grateful I was that my God stopped me before I pulled right up to the intersection. If God had not stopped us, we would have been knocked into on-coming traffic. As it was, when the wreck was over, my car was sitting just slightly under the red light. Not one car was moving. God stopped them all and prevented us from being injured or killed. Whoa! The most non-sleeping baby on the planet slept through the whole episode.

The paramedics and the firefighters arrived almost immediately. They insisted that we go to the hospital with the baby to be looked over. They explained that the level of impact was so strong from the rear-end collision that there might be internal injuries to one or all of us. Amazingly, Cynthia was okay also. There were no cell phones then, but, Loretta,

Cynthia's mother, arrived on the scene fairly quickly. Loretta Cadwell was our first sitter who kept the baby when I was in class. When she saw the other car, she also insisted that we go to the hospital, and went with us. Our car barely had a scratch, but was towed because of some weird internal noise in the engine when it was turned on.

At the hospital, the doctor determined the baby and Cynthia to be unharmed. However, there was a laboratory technician that kept asking me if I were pregnant before he did anything. I kept responding I was not. "I just want to take my baby home", I said. Yet, for no apparent reason, he kept insisting that I have a pregnancy test before giving me an ex-ray. I really can't even articulate the weird badgering this man gave me about having a pregnancy test and not an ex-ray. I now know he was a God-sent messenger – an angel in my room.

Finally, with a conjured up pleasantness and a smile, I said, "I PROMISE. I'm not pregnant. What I am is exhausted and exasperated. My baby is exhausted (though he slept through the whole thing). I just want to go home, feed him, and get him settled. I have homework to do and diapers to wash. However, if it will make you feel better, and you can do whatever you need to do, so we can get out of here, fine. I will have the test and then the ex-ray. But, nothing is broken and I'm not pregnant. I just had a baby. I really can't have any more children. We just want to go home."

Well! When the tests came back, guess what? YES! That's right. I was pregnant. The word shocked does not even begin to define my state of being when the doctor told me the results. Little gown and all, I jumped off the table and ran down the hall, in total disbelief and shock to tell my friend Loretta, and attempt to determine if it was all a dream. A baby was there. We were pregnant, again. What? How?

It was an unfathomable set of miracles whose details I had to share with my husband when the baby and I returned home. How best to do that was the question. George was working in California for the week and I knew both the accident and the well-being of our son would cause him concern. I also had to relay the fact that another baby was coming. You know that call you don't want to make about an accident, even though things could have been a whole lot worse? It was the accident that really was an incredible blessing that revealed the impossible. That's the call I made. Another child... God's Grace is more than amazing.

Do you remember or have you heard about the times when a long distance call was some astronomical charge by the minute? That call was from the east coast to the west coast during that time – 36 years ago. Back then, our telephone bill was easily $300-$400 per month with long distance charges. That one call turned out to be about a $50 conversation, with about half of those dollars paid for silence that travelled across the wires strung over the landscape. I remember that I repeated myself a lot because George couldn't believe the news either. Both of us agreed that it was most unbelievable how God defied the odds of medical science, again, so soon. God has the authority to do so, we know. The periodic silence on the call concerned me that Daddy passed out; but he processed the blessing, too.

Of necessity, I switched obstetricians to one closer in our neighborhood. While I missed Dr. Fabro terribly, the new doctors were extremely competent and accommodating also. Logistically, it was difficult for me to get our infant son and me dressed, drive the 30 miles into the District, in traffic, and find parking. However, being a new Mom was not the sole reason that I was led to find a doctor closer to home. We were concerned about problems associated with the fibroids posing difficulties in major traffic delays, which turned out to be valid concerns.

In the first trimester, my new doctors discovered that there was a placental abruption. That means that the placenta did not attach to the wall of the uterus properly. On top of that, my old trouble makers, the fibroid tumors, were raging again. When the placenta does not attach properly, it can cause uterine contractions, bleeding, and abdominal pain. I had all three. The oxygen supply to the baby can be prevented, as well as the supply of food that is needed for the health of the baby.

One of the potential causes of placental abruption is trauma to the abdomen or problems associated with prior pregnancies. I had both. It took me 37 years to realize that accident was both a blessing and an attack of the enemy. It was a blessing because we didn't die that day and we found out about our new surprise blessing. It was an attack because the accident and tumors made it next to impossible to carry the baby to full term. The doctors were obligated to tell me about the dire circumstances that this condition prompted. They spoke of the possibility of spontaneous abortion because of the contractions, and the potential of death – both of the baby and me. If the baby survived, though they didn't seem to believe the baby would, there could be long-term damages because of inadequate nutrition and oxygen deprivation.

There is no way to re-attach the placenta. I made the decision to trust God. The doctors required complete bed rest with regular monitoring. One of those was impossible with an infant, no family on the scene, and a beloved husband who worked 12-16 hour days or travelled out of town. By then, George was working at Coopers & Lybrand, one of the Big Eight Accounting Firms, as a Management Consultant. Once again, it was a major break for him from God. We would just believe God and wait the gestation process out. Faith kept growing, day by day.

I finished the fall semester of graduate school, very successfully, but barely. George, the doctor, and I made the decision that I would not enroll for the spring semester at Howard. God brought us through all the challenges with the first baby, and we just believed God would do that again. There was no reason to risk any of us further, especially the new baby. I found it easier on me to keep the scary details between God, George and me. That way, the full details somehow seemed less scary. So, we behaved as if everything about the pregnancy was normal. It was not. It was extremely dangerous.

Worldwide, one in 100 pregnant women experience placental disruption. About 25 percent of those disruptions threaten the life of the baby and mother. I was the one in the 100. Our baby and I were the ones, together, in the 25 percent who "they" said possibly would not make it. To know these statistics was disarming then, but they are amazing now. God kept us. The additional challenge was that we already had an infant for whom we had to provide loving and attentive care.

One of the things that caused me quiet concern that I kept to myself, was how seldom the baby moved. Satan tempted me to be afraid. I could totally sense that endless taunting from the enemy. I knew that fear operated against our faith and us. Spiritual warfare was in full presentation and I knew it. God just took care of us. The dangerous contractions happened all the time. That was not good.

I understood what the doctors told me. There was very little space for the baby to move in there because of the tumors that were also being squeezed. So, there were long intervals of time, days, when there was no movement of the baby. I had to trust God. I answered my husband with edifying comments when inquiries were made about how I felt. The baby and I talked to each other a great deal of the time. On this leg of the journey, a different kind of scary activated more faith for me, but a different kind of faith. It is written:

2 Timothy 1:7 – "For God hath not given us the spirit of fear; but of power, and of love, and of a sound mind."

Fear is turned to positive awe and worship when we learn to trust the only One who can help us – God! Faith works from the inside out. That was exactly where I needed faith to be, inside of me with the baby to work things out.

Promptly, on July 2, John E. Miller entered the Miller family and the world. The labor was short, comparatively speaking. It was like eight hours, opposed to endless days that turned to weeks the first time. By the time John was born, pain was a mainstay of my existence. It had become a regular part of my life for almost 18 months combined between two pregnancies. Though once more, I was told about the urgency for the hysterectomy, I didn't have time to think about the tumors, surgery, or any of the other threats of danger, though the threats were all very real.

"Faith through", was my constant command to myself. " Faith through" the circumstance. Since this was definitely our last child, people asked often if we were disappointed that our second son was not a girl. The simple truth is that there was no way that we could do anything but be thankful to God for the unbelievable miracle of our new baby. No one ever knew the whole story, until now. When God gives you a miracle, you just say thank you from the depths of your soul, and all that is within you.

After what baby John went through to share his space with a

grocery list of tumors, I am amazed at how calm he was from the very beginning. He rarely cried. I now know and firmly believe, after all of these years, that God stopped the baby from moving too much. The condition alone was bad enough. The contractions that also squeezed the tumors, and made me feel like a perpetual abdominal toothache, should have caused premature delivery. Who knows what would have happened if the movement were normal. ONLY MY GOD IS IN MY DETAILS!

While all of the blood transfusions were once more very disarming, they were most necessary. The processes replaced almost all of my blood. With every drip, there was this creepy, crawly feeling like a ton of ice-cold ants was going into my body. Things and circumstances that God uses to save us are rarely pleasant to us.

All I know is that our son beat the 60% mortality rate for the condition, despite which he was born. So did I. He has no mental disorders due to oxygen deprivation, or physical abnormalities, as it was suggested there might be. Though proper growth was potentially a problem, he made it here perfectly formed. His disposition was totally peaceful and calm. Without much room to grow, he did grow to a healthy seven plus pounds at delivery. The entire process that God uses to form and birth a baby is beyond our ability to comprehend. Even though humans are gifted to understand some limited dimension of obstetrics, only God knows the full scope. God is Grace.

Musings with God the Holy Spirit!

- The healthy gestation period is critical to the life that is formed and will be birthed.

- Value the process of gestation for dreams and visions, despite the unknown factors that are always lurking.
- The womb of eternity is where God forms us and calls us forth to be God's unique creation.
- Pay attention to the womb which nurtures life.
- There is no malady in the spiritual womb.
- As much attention as possible should be focused on what God has in the womb to birth through us.
- We cannot really see what is going in the formation of the child on a minute by minute basis, but God can.
- Jesus Christ is the true "Son-ogram" Who is able to measure and adjust everything for the baby, during gestation, according to the need.
- God the Holy Spirit creates the perfect spiritual and physical conditions for a healthy, whole, live birth to occur, according to the Will of God.
- Likewise, when God the Holy Spirit is our God, Partner, Guide, Protector, and Deliverer, our visions and dreams grow into reality at God's appointed time.
- I have often pondered the question and resolved it in my own mind and spirit that satan attacks the womb.
- A strong prayer covering with a Holy Spirit Christian church family and believers is very important.
- A baby who survives to birth and the mother who survives to delivery should be celebrated.
- The baby should be dedicated back to God as soon as possible.
- God entrusts us to bring another human into the world and care for the baby.
- We should show reverence to parenting as a unique blessing from God, regardless of circumstances.
- Honor God for the gift of a child.
- Manage gestation and parenting well with fervent prayer.

Chapter 5
Oh God!
The Delivery Is Extreme!

John 16:21 - "A woman giving birth to a child has pain because her time has come; but when her baby is born she forgets the anguish because of her joy that a child is born into the world."

With two babies, who were born just 13 months apart, glued to my hip and arms most of the time, I finished my Masters. George and John went every with me. If they could not go, usually I could not either. They went to the library on the campus of Howard, and in the neighborhood, more than a few times with me. Our two sons were at the graduation, impeccably dressed, with white high-top shoes, and everything that made me smile at God for God's Grace that permitted two miracles to happen for us. George was an absolutely wonderful father and husband. I loved being Mom.

Christmas 1982, we made our regular holiday trip, among many regular trips, to Atlanta. On our drive back to Fairfax, I became very ill. Halfway home, we had to stop and spend the night in a hotel before we continued our trip because of the excruciating pain that punctuated every move. I was convinced that the fibroid tumors were on some kind of rampage. After the birth of each son, the doctors told me that I really needed to schedule the big one – the hysterectomy. However, with two small children, the time never was quite right to have the surgery done. Whether it was convenient or not, it seemed the time had come. I promised George that I would call Dr. Fabro as soon as we returned home to set everything in order, and to schedule the surgery. The need was a long, forgone conclusion.

We had a grand reunion indeed when I met with Dr. Fabro. We were separated for over three years. He was far more than a doctor. He was our faith-partner and trusted friend. So, as good friends do, we just picked up from where we left off, as if the time never elapsed. As far as I was concerned, no one else could do the surgery. He had to be my surgeon. Now, George and I were a family of four. He marveled at the two newest members when he saw them. So did George and I. We shared the blessings we had experienced with him, and his marvelously competent Administrative Assistant, as well. She was also a valuable part of our miracle network; and, always connected me directly to Dr. Fabro, whenever I called, if he didn't pick up the phone himself. We often joked about him doing her job. She was God-sent, too.

When Dr. Fabro finished the examination, he brought George in for the results and consultation. His message seemed to pick right back up where we stopped the last time, too. This time, he seemed much too grave in his countenance as he began.

"Well My Lovely! It is true. The tumors are misbehaving very badly, again. I can see why you were in so much pain. And yes! You must have the surgery, as soon as possible. But that will have to wait a while longer. There is a baby in there", said Dr. Fabro.

AGAIN! Shocked! Speechless! Dumfounded! Unbelievable! Those are all good words to insert here, though totally inadequate to describe the silence in the room that turned to laughter of incredulousness. We are talking about what the extremely competent medical experts said could not happen. Even Dr. Fabro, one very highly skilled expert, could not understand from a medical and scientific point of view how another pregnancy was possible. The array of fibroids also didn't permit birth control pills as an option. Can I just say God navigated everything about the conception and birth of our children? I mean absolutely everything. Say nothing to me about birth control. We knew the answers. All of it was way beyond our ability to comprehend, understand, coordinate, or explain. I have never been surer that God works God's plan in my life. God is God alone!

It was the first week in January 1983. The scenarios were way too familiar, but way different at the same time. Now, there were two toddler boys, aged two and a half, and three and a half years old. They would unknowingly make the journey through the maze of tumor-time-bombs with us, again, in a different manner. Because of the boys, the stakes were much, much higher this time. Precautions were the same, but enhanced in intensity, if that was possible.

Complete bed rest was ordered, but once again impossible to achieve with two children who were so young. Once more, the only thing we could do was to give it over to the Lord and really leave the pregnancy in God's hands. God decided for us. For the first time, I admit, that while I may seem crazy to some, the level of spiritual awareness was greatly enhanced with the birth of each child. My closeness to God was pronounced.

Except for the continuous pain and the multiple crabapples, lemons, tangerines and oranges that protruded and were obvious under the skin, yet in the womb, things were not that bad. The human mind has a plethora of coping skills. And, God has a way of helping us to forget some things, so God can do a new thing for us, through us and to us. That is especially true when it comes to birthing babies in the world. Otherwise, everyone would be an only child, if the mother did not forget the significant event..

Once again, abortion was raised as a medical option, but it was not an option that we would entertain. Once again, the question was raised about who should be saved if things went left. This time, I said the baby should be saved. That was odd, in light of the fact there would be three kids to care for without their Mother. I trusted God.

We made it through the pregnancy. By then, George had started his own Management Consulting firm called Spectrum Consulting Associates, Inc. He took a flight with boys to our parents in Atlanta. They would care for them until the new baby was born. During the last week of my doctor's visits, Dr. Fabro decided that if the baby were not born within a week from that day, he would hospitalize me to induce labor. Labor persisted, almost non-stop. Though the contractions and pain were strong enough in my book to kill an ox, they were not producing the desired result – delivery.

I checked into Columbia Hospital for Women in Washington to begin inducement. Once again, Dr. Fabro advised us that it would be best for the baby to come on its own, but he had to induce labor. A Cesarean was the last option for me because of the tumors. For three days, Pitocin was pumped into my veins. Each day, for three days, the medical team took me down to labor and delivery the first thing every morning, around seven a.m., and returned me to my room around five p.m.

The contractions were massive, but useless. The danger of inducement was that the baby's respiration and heart rate could drop. That they did – drastically - by the end of the third day. The emergency Cesarean had to take place. All options were gone. I remember feeling so sad for George and Dr. Fabro. The unknown weighed heavily upon them, and it was very obvious. The hour arrived. Indeed, as the Bible says in 2 Kings 19:3, "we had come to the hour of birth and there was no strength to deliver."

As they rolled me pass the nurses station, really quickly, but in some kind of surreal slow motion, I saw a long black, leather binder that opened lengthwise like a business checkbook propped against the book rack on the counter. On the front of the binder were gold letters that literally jumped out at me. The words that I read said "**Death Record**". They were like piercing daggers! Softly, I said, "Jesus rebukes that."

I knew the taunting presence of the enemy attempted to surround me with fear. I also knew that the presence and power of God were there, too, over everything. The evidence was there that this was definitely spiritual warfare of the deepest kind. I had no idea how entrenched the warfare would be. The only way that I can describe that moment is to say God had me on spiritual lockdown. Silently, I said to God, "I am not going in there". That meant that though I was in a weakened and frail condition, and up against the forces of hell, they would not add my name to the Death Record. I remained in spiritual lockdown mode. All I had to do was hold onto my faith and not panic.

When we reached the Operating Room, Dr. Fabro and George greeted me in hospital scrubs. George was in the delivery room for the birth of our two sons. Although this was a Cesarean birth, he was to be present in the room for the birth of this baby, also. He and Dr. Fabro went to scrub up for the surgery, as they rolled me into the operating room.

I remember that operating room to this day. I remember the cavalier nurses and anesthesiologist who were present. They talked incessantly about their personal lives, like I was not present, as they marked my spine for the epidural. The epidural would numb my body from the waist downward. I remember telling them that the shots preceding the epidural to make it less painful weren't working. They basically ignored me, and kept talking. I remembered the dentist from my childhood and another one from my young adult years who told me they hoped I never had to have major surgery because it was almost impossible to numb me. Those words became reality for me.

The anesthesiologist inserted the needle at roughly the same point of previous injections for George and John. On rainy days I could feel the spots hurting which I ignored. The nurses and anesthesiologist talked about their dates the past weekend, and rudely gave me instructions not to move. I felt the initial cold trickle of medicine that would block all feeling in my body from the waist down, supposedly. All of a sudden, something went terribly wrong. The anesthesia that was supposed to only block the lower part of my body went down and up. I could feel it knocking out my heart and lungs. The only thing I can compare it to is the way you pump air into a tire. A human implosion was underway. I knew the medicine was traveling fast, but in slow motion, at the same time. God corrected for the error and gave me the presence of mind to do something.

"Oh My God! I'm dying", I said to the Lord, though no one else could hear me. Suddenly, I felt the pressure rise, and it kept rising, as all the systems of my body shut down in a power failure. Like a tire being over filled with too much air, all the way up to my shoulders, life was being knocked out. I realized if I didn't hold on to my faith and consciousness that would be it. I was drowning in the air pressure; or shut down like a building was imploding; or all of my circuitry was shut off. The numbness, the pressure, the imploding, or total electrical failure was literally up to my nose when God led me to spell! G O D! G O D! G O D! God took control. I called. Almighty God answered.

The spiritual me was zoomed up to the ceiling. There, in the ceiling, I hovered, though conscious of everything that was transpiring in the room. I could see when Dr. Fabro burst into the room. At first, he was giving George instructions or answers just outside the room, as they waited to come in for the delivery. Then, he abruptly left George, who was terrified and alone, outside the OR, with no explanation of what was happening. As I zoomed out and up to the ceiling, I simultaneously heard Dr. Fabro call out to me. "OH, MY GOD! NOOO! Hold on My Lovely! Hold on! Please hold on", he said. I heard Dr. Fabro,

They snatched my head back and ran what felt like an ice-cold, iron pipe down my throat. I felt every bit of it. In some strange interplay of consciousness, I remember thinking how very cold the steel pipe was, even though I am still not sure if the pipe was steel at all. At the same time, my spirit travelled through this unimaginably beautiful, perfect garden. I realized that I crossed the dimension or chasm between this world and the next, heaven. Suddenly there, I was not alone. I recognized the Indescribable Presence with me. I knew the Presence was God. The enormous, gargantuan love and the perfect peace that surpasses all understanding that emanated from God were there, too.

Although I could not see God's face, to be in God's Presence was beyond comprehension. The feeling was like being with all of my closest loved ones, family and friends, from every stage of my life, compounded in one Person, but more. The feeling was like we met in God's Presence for dinner at a really special place that embraced absolute Truth and Love. I "knew in my knowing" (the only way I can articulate the encounter) that the most remarkable knowledge came directly from God, at that moment. That knowledge was appropriate only for that place. Time was suspended or non-existent. Kairos, God's time, was all that there was. We were in the midst of eternity.

There was another presence that emotionally embraced me. I "knew in my knowing" that the other presence was an angel who took on the form and essence of my maternal Grandmother. My Grandmother entered heaven on July 5, 1966. After much seeking for understanding that God later let me "know in my knowing" that the angel assumed that form as my Grandmother, so I would not be afraid. That is why I gladly went with them; through the portal of time; into Eternity and into the "Garden".

The Garden seemed like an entrance place, with something even more spectacular beyond it, but a part of it. We went through The Gate. I was not afraid at all. In fact, what I later perceived as Paradise, greatly appealed to all of my spirit and soul. Physical bodies were non-existent, just the essence of them, spirits. With some unseen, gentle, caressing, magnetic force, I was drawn into an incredibly beautiful place, absent of anything temporal or transitory like time. I knew where we were, and who the Companions were who escorted me into the power of the eternal. Can we say that eternity is a powerful state of being? YES!

In the natural realm, when Dr. Fabro rushed into the room, he quickly zipped across my abdomen vertically. What happened was all the worst of what he thought could happen. I felt the knife go through the layers of my flesh. The numbness from the epidural did not set in. The warning about cutting a fibroid and me bleeding to death went out the window. Dr. Fabro knew I was dying and went for the baby. I learned later that he broke his own record for a C-Section delivery. It took 18 seconds, he told me, to get in there and get the baby out. I was definitely caught between two worlds – life and afterlife. The scalpel hurt and didn't hurt.

There was a young Resident or Fellow, Dr. Oliver Kreitman, who assisted Dr. Fabro. He was very skilled and impacted me significantly when I first met him. No doubt, this young doctor received some knowledge from the experience that books and classes could never teach him. I knew that he was a particularly gifted doctor because he was gifted to work with the phenomenal Dr. Fabro. God chose Dr. Kreitman to be there. The connection that was needed was made. We would meet again. Consciousness of life and an after-life experience occurred together.

My spirit and soul felt the absolute peace and perfection in the most incredible Garden, as we moved in it. There was no fear, only the infinite best and absolute good existed with everything. This was heaven. I could smell the scent of jasmine that I would later smell on earth, many times. Then! I heard the baby cry. I remember the Biblical account that Moses cried at just the right moment. That cry of our baby halted me in the transition process. The cry was far away, yet near. It was to me even as the cry of Moses when Pharaoh's daughter rescued him from the bulrushes. I spoke to God and my Grandmother (angel) through my mind, thought to thought, without words. The Light and Love that emanated from God, at that moment, were absolutely phenomenal and unspeakable beauty.

"I have to go back. He (my husband) can't take care of them (three children) without me. I have to go back", I said only with my thoughts. They understood what my spirit said, clearly and distinctly, as I spoke, without words. God released me.

Back in the operating room, I sensed they were pulling the sheet up over me because I was dead. Still unconscious, I couldn't understand why they were doing that. I began to fight to let them know not to cover me up. "I'm not dead. I am alive", I said with my thoughts. I started to move my two middle fingers, the only part of my body that I could move. Ironically, prior to that point, I was not able to use those two fingers on my right hand. I accidently burned them through to the bone to keep our oldest son from grabbing a hot pan. At the time, he was in his walker, and charged for the open oven door. I heard Dr. Fabro say, "She's coming back. She's coming back." A lot of commotion proceeded.

Only when I saw my husband did I know for sure that the episode was over. I was alive. George was so distraught that I will always feel badly that he went through that ordeal of uncertainty. He stood just beyond the doors to the OR the whole time that I was in crisis without knowing what was going on. He missed the birth of his daughter. It was a while before either of us knew the baby was a girl. One of the nurses who was in the operating room didn't know either. They rushed the baby out to do procedures, so quickly. We called Atlanta as soon as I got in the recovery room. They were still working on the baby. George gave my Mama and Daddy the details about what happened, but told them I was alright.

When he put me on the phone, I spoke with this little teeny tiny voice of a three year old kid, the same way I talked to him. I felt exuberance in my mind and spirit that I had never felt before. The feeling was a result of the out-of-body experience. To this day, I don't know what my presenting myself as a little child was about. I learned later that the sound of that voice, whatever it was, frightened my Mother to no end. She in turn frightened our sons, George and John, who were expecting to hear about their new sibling. The news they received was not exactly the news my parents wanted to hear. As always, my Daddy, though also distraught, took control and diffused the panic, as always.

The anesthesiologist paid me more than a few visits in the recovery room, and later in my hospital room. The first and second visits were part of the protocol following surgery. The other visits and her approach afterwards were not. The Gift of

Discernment has always served me well. I knew she feared a lawsuit. There I was in the process of recovery. She was concerned about what I would do regarding the fact that she almost killed our baby and me because of negligence. She made conditions right for an attack of the enemy. Our conversation was strained at best.

For the next seven days, I was in the hospital. What seemed like endless blood transfusions were administered. The biggest health issue for me was the doctor's inability to stabilize my blood pressure, respiration, and heart rate. I had to regain the use of my legs, but those were very small issues to me. Once more, God triumphed. It seemed that quite a bit of conversation went on around the hospital about the birth of our daughter I was told. Apparently, most of the hospital staff heard what happened and quite a few came by to say so. The opportunity to testify was soothing for me. I was hooked up to all kinds of medication, monitors and machines. (Additional details of this story are included in *Angels in My Room!*) We named our baby girl Mikah, which is the feminized version of the Biblical Micah, whose name means, "Who is like God".

The will of God prevailed. God chose both of us, the baby and me, and permitted both of us to live. The experience changed our lives forever. I cherished the time to share the out-of-body experience with anyone who would listen. However, many people did not believe me. My whole spirit, soul, and mind were greatly expanded; and I didn't know how to get them back in my body. Needless to say, neither did anyone else; nor did many seem to understand. After a while , I learned to be silent on the subject. I also learned a greater truth about the scripture that would forever inform my life and witness. It is written:

Deuteronomy 30:19-20 – " I call heaven and earth to record this day against you, that I have set before you life and death, blessing, and cursing: therefore choose life, that both thou and thy seed may live: That thou may love the Lord thy God, and that thou may obey his voice, and that thou mayest cleave unto him: for he is thy life, and the length of thy days: that thou mayest dwell in the land which the Lord sware unto thy fathers, to Abraham, to Isaac, and to Jacob to give them."

I always believed that I would die at the age of 33 because that was the age at which Jesus was crucified on the Cross. Even that thought was a prophetic warning.   That was almost a self-fulfilling prophecy. At 33 years and three months old, I came as close to death as one can come, and live to tell about it. The postpartum recovery was amazing. In a real way, my mind, soul and spirit were still in supernatural suspension. No longer am I bothered that people did not or do not believe me

The six weeks follow-up visit to see Dr. Fabro was amazing, but difficult to explain. That time is yet among the most spiritual moments in my life. God threw me a life line through him. The four of us, Dr. Fabro, Dr. Kreitmann, George, and I, were a part of some major miracle and we all knew that. We had to process the birth, for Dr. Fabro's benefit and mine. He explained his thoughts and memory about my near-death, out-of-body experience.

With his wonderful accent, Dr. Fabro said, "I talked to your spirit. I knew your spirit could hear me. I was not talking out loud. I talked to your spirit." To learn that was so very profoundly gratifying for me. What I learned that day was how Dr. Fabro used his voice to help me maintain some consciousness of this life, so that I was able to hear the baby cry. Dr. Fabro could not believe that I saw the Death Register when I described it to him. He said,

"Oh my God! That is never, ever visible. How did that happen?" How did that happen, indeed? I clearly got the message.

Somehow, God helped me to know the value of that encounter with God to my own life. My desire was to let people know about the power of God. I wanted to share over and over again how God is concerned and will manage every detail of our lives, if we give our lives to Jesus.

The after-effects of the out-of-body experience kept me floating in some surreal context, while going about our daily routine of parenthood. I remained hyper-sensitive to the spirit world from that point forward. To engage in small talk was never my strong suit. After that experience, trivia and things became more superfluous than ever. We were so delighted and blessed that God gave our family additional gifts of life, hers and mine,

As often as possible, we should surrender our will and everything about us to God. The deep generosity of God's grace reveals God's thoughts, even the secret things to God's anointed, according to Jeremiah 33:3, Daniel 2:22 and Luke 8:17. God directs this cosmic drama called life, and is well aware of each act in the drama and every character in it. We panic when we permit our mind, our thoughts, and our actions to move ahead of God. God blesses us. It is written:

Jeremiah 33:3 – "Call unto Me, and I will answer thee, and shew thee great and mighty things, which thou knowest not."

Daniel 2:22 – "He reveals the deep and secret things: He knoweth what is in the darkness, and the light dwelleth with Him."

Luke 8:17 – "For nothing is secret that shall not be made manifest; neither anything hid that shall not be known and come abroad."

Musing with God the Holy Spirit!

- GOD IS GOD!.
- Stay ready to go with Jesus, wherever Jesus leads us, or whenever Jesus returns.
- God still works God-sized Miracles.
- God is our Loving Father Who does all things perfectly that pertain to us.
- Everything God gives and does are perfect.
- God's vision is fulfilled according to God's appointed time.
- The enemy is hell-bent on destroying that child that God gives and assigns for Kingdom work.
- Likewise, the enemy is hell-bent on turning the vision that God gave you into a nightmare.
- Prayer and the deliberate study of the Word of Almighty God are paramount for victory.
- Frustration with God's gift may be a sign that you are attempting to control the outcome.
- If God is in control, success is our reward.
- If we put ourselves in control, the outcome is potentially another self-destructive straw. Remember the camel.
- The power of God exceeds every act of satan.
- God calls us before God placed us in the womb.
- God does not need our approval for anything, including the birth of a baby.
- Babies should always remind us of God's love.
- Babies are God's signature on c

Chapter 6
Oh God!
I Surrender All!

Romans 8:26-27 - "Likewise the Spirit also helpeth our infirmities: for we know not what we should pray for as we ought: but the Spirit maketh intercession for us with groanings which cannot be uttered. And He that searcheth knoweth the mind of the Spirit, because He maketh intercession for the saints according to the will of God."

As often as possible, we should surrender our lives, and everyone and everything in our lives to God the Holy Spirit Who is present with us now; and reveals the deep generosity of God's grace to share God's thoughts with us. God directs this cosmic drama called life. The sooner we recognize and accept that fact, the better off we are. Surrender to God is not optional, but obligatory because of our faith in the God of Jesus Christ.

Time arrived when we enrolled our sons, George and John, in the Springs Montessori School. I was able to focus my attention exclusively on Mikah, the new baby, for a few hours. They began classes after Labor Day in 1983, less than a month after I was released from the hospital. So much for that ten-week recovery period upon which the doctor insisted that I take. Even with our two Mothers and a Grandmother, over the course of six weeks, rest was not possible. They were tree of the best Christians,

Mothers, cooks, caregivers, ever. The boys needed my attention.

One October evening, we were busy with our new routine as a family of five. Since we were yet in the physical recovery and adjustment mode to our new way of life, managing our newly configured family was challenging to say the least. That day was one of the rare moments when George was home because he took a vacation day to spend with us. Our Mothers were gone back to Atlanta, and we settled into our new routine. It was a great day.

After an unusually early dinner, George and John asked if they could go outside to ride their bikes for a little while. It was still very light outside. They knew the rules. "Stay in sight – three houses to the left and three houses to the right." That gave them an ample distance to ride back and forth. I consented. When they were outside, I formed the habit of watching them from the kitchen windows, and the storm door with the glass was always open. Yet, in a matter of a few minutes, after they went out, John rushed in the house, and made a statement in a way that I knew something was very wrong.

"Mommy, I can't find George", he said, panic stricken. "What do you mean, you can't find George", I said, as I hurried out the kitchen door.

I looked at George's bike under the huge oak tree in the center of the front yard. The wheels were still spinning. It was a surreal image and moment that I will never forget. The image seemed to be a frightful scene from a movie that someone cut and pasted into our lives without our permission. As best I could, I calmly questioned John and took him in the house to his Dad. I ran up and down the street and knocked on our neighbors' doors. Most of them were home, but none of them or their kids had seen George.

I went inside and told my husband what happened, and dialed

911. The Fairfax County Police swooped in almost as soon as I hung up the phone. Officers were everywhere, as the fall evening began to set in. Everything was calm or at least we attempted to be, just after the test that we passed in the childbirth with Mikah. Calmness gave way. We were beyond distraught as the police officer interrogated George and me. Yet, we held on to our faith. Neighbors came in and out.

The whole subdivision searched. There were people on bikes, kids on skateboards, and people driving around in their cars. As the sun began to set, high intensity lighting was set up. People combed the neighborhood with flashlights. The scene was unbelievable, then and now, how our neighbors banded together. We bought our home and moved in that April before George was born. Only one family who lived across the street moved because we moved in. The Maneys, the Teasdales, the Schulsteads, and the Coopers are still family to this day. The residents of our community largely worked at the Pentagon, and were high-ranking government and military officials. We were the only minorities in the subdivision; and George was an entrepreneur, not military or government employee. Only the children from Kings Park West went to that school. The neighbors and police were very thorough in their search.

Around 10:00 p.m., after over five hours of searching, I went outside to stand under the night sky. That way I felt the direct connect with God. I began to pray to the Lord; dropped to my knees on the ground; and then lay prostrate before God to plead our case. My prayer to God was to remind God that our son was terribly afraid of the dark. Engulfed in tears and agony, I held the worse conversation of my life with God. That was my " Sarah's heart break for Isaac and Abraham" moment, when we surrender to God that which is highly valued and treasured. Surely, God did not give George to us to permit the enemy to take him. Bewilderment and devastation wrung our hearts.

In fervent prayer, I said to God, "You know that he is terrified of the dark. I don't believe You brought us through all of that with his birth to bring us to this. But, if You permitted someone to take him, I ask You to please take him quickly to be with You. I give George back to You. Please don't let him be hurt or afraid. Take him. Thank You God. In Jesus' Name, I pray. Amen!" My heart plummeted.

The police sent for me to come inside. They sat me down at the kitchen table. They calmly said to me once more that I should call my family in Atlanta and my Pastor. They asked for a photo so they could make the 11:00 news. I just couldn't do it. I all but lost consciousness, but I could not give the Officer a photo. "No matter how diligent I was to protect them, I failed. God is in control. Thy will be done." Those were the thoughts that ran through my mind on a continuous loop. The baby slept the whole time.

I kept attempting to send John to another room, so he would not be distraught or affected worse in the long term, if things worked out badly. He would not leave. As the police kept insisting on the photo and the phone calls, John said these words. "I'm going to go get my brother." Shortly, he returned through the sliding doors on the lower level where we were talking to the police. His brother was with him. We could not believe who we saw before us. THANK YOU GOD!!!

Our little four-years old George was literally covered in mud, from head to toe, like he had been buried somewhere. Neither the police nor his Dad or I could believe what we saw and heard. He kept acting like he was the news anchor Ed Bradley on the scene of this event, with a pretend microphone in his hand. The police looked at us very strangely, signifying something crazy was going on. His Dad was instructed to take George into the bathroom to check him. There was no way that the police believed the story George told us that he was hiding in the tall shrubbery on the side of the house. They literally combed every inch of our property, surrounding property, and everywhere possible in our community. Those officers and all the neighbors were beyond wonderful, diligent, and more than thoroughly precise. precise, an

I will always say something occurred during those five hours that I yet think was some other kind of supernatural thing, beyond the normal. The specifics of that eventful evening and night can never be proved. They don't need to be. All I know is that day I fully surrendered our children to God, again, and everything about our lives. Each of them was given back to God in infancy.

In infancy, we took George and John back to Atlanta where Reverend Dr. Julius C. Williams Christened them at Flipper Temple A.M.E. Church. Mikah was later dedicated to the Lord at Metropolitan Baptist Church in Washington. But that night, if I did not understand anything else about how or why that event happened, I know that I really gave them to God, again, all of them, throughout all generations. I vowed that for my role in their lives, they would be raised as disciples of Jesus Christ. Absolutely everything was surrendered to God. I committed to disciple them as a parent. God would give what I gave to God back to me to train them for God's service. The Holy Word is true. It is written:

Romans 8:3 – "What shall we then say to these things? If God is for us, who can be against us?"

We have to know the value of this verse and indeed every verse in the rest of Romans 8, and the value of every word of every verse in the entire Holy Bible. We don't always see how things are working together for our good. However, critical to that "good" becoming our reality is the act of surrender. Surrender means that God must be totally in control, because God is, whether we believe it or not. Through all of the challenges to give birth or bring children into the world, I learned that the best way to surrender is to recall the past in the context of our present. We will see Jesus in the midst of things, good or not so good at the time that will ultimately prove to be for our good. The grace of God gets us to the refrain that says, "It's all good!"

The denotative meaning of surrender lists submission as a synonym. However, I painfully learned from this heart wrenching experience that there is a significant difference between being submitted to God and totally surrendered to God. To totally surrender to God meant that I gave up all rights to and control of anything, everything, and everybody, including our children. It meant to surrender myself, totally and completely to God's will and authority.

The God to Whom I surrendered is the Sole Authority in my life. That required me to embrace God's love for me differently from that point on; and to believe emphatically that God works on our best interest. God is not our opponent. I later realized how I unknowingly opposed the will of God for my life in my feeble attempt to retain some control. The authority over my life, and everything and every person in my life, who comes and who is removed, was given to God, again. I would not take it back, either consciously or unconsciously. The act of falling to the ground that night was my act of surrender that would govern the rest of my days here on terra firma.

As always, while we move in our day-to-day activities, we should remember that God already wrote our individual stories in eternity. God orchestrates our stories to play out in the earth realm according to God's plan for us. That plan is for God's glory and for our good, if we permit. That is why it is so important to stay well connected with God the Holy Spirit. We will hear God's voice, even if we don't like what God says, sometimes.

I knew without a doubt that the call of God to preach the Gospel was closing in on me. I wanted so desperately to do God's will, since childhood. However, I wanted to act like either God or I made a mistake. I knew better. The other problem was that I set limits on God. Yet, there was nothing else I could offer God and hope God would be satisfied.

"The Way" became a lot more narrow. God makes room for escape from temptation, but not from God or God's call on our lives. We disobey God at the risk of our own perishing. God speaks in unlimited ways. Expect to hear, listen and obey God's Voice, even though God may speak to us through other people. God speaks volumes to us from God's Holy Word. The path for God's truth to reavh us is unlimited. Oh the light and power of the Truth that sets us free when we are obedient. That same Truth becomes our albatross if we are disobedient. All of it, had become too much, including Grace and gratitude which overwhelmed me.

Following my final checkup with Dr. Fabro, I made an appointment to meet with our Pastor, Dr. H. Beecher Hicks, Jr. at Metropolitan Baptist Church in Washington, D.C. Let me say that another way because I really want you to sense my exasperation. I fervently and honestly say to you that the world and all of life were way "too much with me", to twist slightly the saying from the poet William Wordsworth. My God-view expanded beyond my ability to take hold of it and manage it. I am still not clear if we can or should manage our God-view, as I call it; or continue to expand that view; maybe both. I needed to go to the House of God, even if it was on a Thursday. God moved.

My testimony about the miraculous birth made me want to offer myself to God even more than ever. Thoughts of sharing the love of God with others were both indiscriminately satiating and strangling at the same time. I wanted to tell everyone about the Trinity. I always had. So did every Christian, I thought. There was nothing that I possessed that was so great, I reasoned. Yet, the meeting was scheduled with the Pastor for the Miller's blessed Miracle and me.

God had always laid a desire on my heart to help expand the children's "program" in Church, even when I was a child myself. I wanted to help improve the children's "program" at Metropolitan, which at the time was active, but minimal, and dwindling. George and I were one of the very few young couples in the very historic and powerful Metropolitan Baptist Church at the time. The Church was in transition. Christ, the people were beautiful and accomplished. We loved the people.

Through relationship with the Triune God, because of Christ who is the Messiah King, through God the Holy Spirit, the Church of Jesus Christ and family were and yet are the reason for everything in my life, all of my life. Any moment away from Church even to give birth was painful. Since we now had three children of our own, God inspired me to do the next thing that would forever change my life. Can I just say, in a way, though completely naïve to the movement of God's providence, I wanted to do absolutely ANYTHING at all to serve God. I would be the custodial servant and clean dust and cobwebs off the ceiling.

God is my EVERYTHING who gives me a husband who God requires, as a Christian, to behave like Jesus toward me, to love and care for me in this life. Because God gave that husband to me, who I love and respect, I have no difficulty in my life to submit to him. and sons and daughters to parent. That is the way see God, even now. The child-like wonder was there. God grew as I grew, at my spiritually immature stage of life. That is how I felt. The reality is, that God is immediately massive, beyond our comprehension; while at the same time intricately engaged with God's daughters and sons. God prepares us to do everything that God calls us to do and be. The choice is always ours to obey or disobey.

We are the creation. So many times, we present ourselves as some paragon of virtuous logistics. We behave and respond as if we have all the answer to all the whys that life and living bring. God makes the decision for each and every human who exists, ever existed, or will exist. The great gift of "free will" which God gave us should be humbly expressed in an absolute covenant to let God be God in our lives. God is God, a

Musings with God the Holy Spirit!

- What God calls us to do has eternal significance, beyond our comprehension and our time frame.
- Only the God of Jesus Christ can choreograph the ebb and flow of life, the obedience of nature, and the arrogance of humankind in such a way that God works God's plan.
- God is able to conduct the elements of time on the stringed instruments of eternity to produce a melodious sound of victory in the silence of our tears.
- God is Absolute Wisdom Who is able to perfect a perfect plan through an imperfect people.
- God's plan is fully loaded with actions that God already performed for us.
- We are challenged to grow, especially in the midst of adversity, to receive what God provides.
- Faith maximizes the potential in us that carries the seed.

Chapter 7
Oh God!
The Narrow Way Narrows!

Luke 12:48 - "...For unto whomsoever much is given, of him shall much be required; and to whom men have committed much, of him they will ask the more."

In retrospect, from where I sit 33 years later, what God the Holy Spirit revealed to me is that much like the Azusa Street Revival that lasted from 1906-1917, all of us in the Church of Jesus Christ were participants in a major move of God. That movement seems to have commenced around 1979/1980 and lasted to the year 2000. My expertise on this stream of thought lacks the credibility of scholarship. However, I believe that as we progressed toward the 21st century, the movement of God the Holy Spirit was akin to the Azusa Street Revival, and the Church of Jesus Christ did not really acknowledge the movement very well. We are able to identify the movement retrospectively. Certainly, you may draw your own conclusions.

At that meeting, I gave my testimony to Pastor Hicks about my out-of-body experience and the whole event that occurred when Mikah was born. He carefully listened; and offered wise counsel. God gave me clear instructions that I was to serve in ministry, and I shared that with the Pastor. In the context of our discussion, Dr. Hicks laid out the needs of the Church regarding youth. NO specific details on how to proceed were all given. What was the bottom line? I said yes. I wasn't sure from whence that yes to draft the proposal for a youth ministry came; or where my yes would lead in the process. The only thing that was certain was that I knew that I trusted God, and it would seem that Pastor Hicks trusted where God would lead me to begin the new work. This was NOT a "program", God the Holy Spirit revealed to me. The Holy Spirit had already designed the proposed Metropolitan Baptist Church Youth Ministries in Eternity. I would not trifle with that decision. I did not know what to do or how to do it. That was most impressive. God worked with my willingness to do what God says, despite my ignorance. Strangely enough, ignorance was the most blissful state I had ever known.

The language we were to use, according to the Angel Messengers, was very important to give new life to the new infant ministry. I went home to write the vision for the new ministry that God gave me in rapid fire. Obedience has Godly benefits. At that moment, I could hear God better than ever in my life. God definitely spoke. I listened. I wrote. Even though I constantly gave recommendations to our childhood Pastor about different ideas and "programs", I don't remember ever being led to receive a vision or lead anything of this magnitude in the Church before.

I repeat. I did not know how to do anything that God directed me to do. Why did God do that to me so often? Nor did I know how to do any of the things that God told me would follow. But, I trusted God with the direction; and appreciated Dr. Hicks' willingness and desire for God to create ministry through me. The vision was completely bold and beyond me. I knew it came from God, as it began to traverse my mind almost immediately. Therefore, I totally depended on God Who assembled the team of Church parents and members to make the work happen. The wheels were grinding, as the angels of God greased the axle.

In a matter of a few hours, as I mused and meditated with the Lord God, between picking up the two sons from Montessori, making lunch and dinner, and changing diapers on the newborn baby girl, God gave me an outstanding model for what would become the new Youth Ministries of Metropolitan Baptist Church, including the name and organization. The process happened unbelievably fast. In many ways, God's revolutionary move was in action that we would experience many times in days, weeks, months, and years to come. Spiritual motivation superseded the trepidation of my flesh. In other words, faith trumped fear.

The vision for the ministry was a comprehensive approach for children from six weeks old to 18 years of age, and their parents. Therefore, the design included 50 plus components. Dr. Hicks approved the plan God gave me through the vision. Reflection says it really was a vision that God gave when I was a youth with no way to make it happen. The time for fulfillment had not yet come. God calls us early and then prepares us for the assignment.

Within a matter of days, I agreed to come on staff as the Volunteer Youth Director who received a stipend of $75 a month. The stipend really didn't even pay for the cost of the gas I needed to get back and forth to the Church from Fairfax. God worked me into a position without my knowledge. With high gas prices, that $75 was about three tanks of gas. I lived 30 miles away and drove a gas-guzzling Monte Carlo. (I have to laugh right here.) George subsidized the rest. God moved me to that inescapable position where the narrow way that I call Redemption Road narrowed even more. My movement was under the remote control of God. Pastor Hicks appointed me to the Board of Christian Education.

The first act of business that God instructed me to conduct was personal prayer and fasting. Then God led me to go out the back door of the Church, one morning, and walk through the back door of Garrison Elementary School behind us. I did not have an appointment, but the principal received me and the offer to help like we did have an appointment. We talked at length about the needs of the faculty and students. A priceless, beneficial relationship was advanced with her and the faculty that tremendously blessed the children with a multitude of services. Our ministry there was extremely viable. The Church and school became intertwined through our services to them. Community outreach and involvement was our ministry design which we constantly embraced.

Almost every Saturday, Mrs. Gladiola McDaniel and her sons and grandchildren, along with Daisy Maggette and her daughters, and I would witness door to door in the community. The more we walked the streets to introduce Jesus, invite our neighbors to worship, and tell them about Youth Ministries, the more God revealed about my work. It is more than amazing and amusing now that we started our Youth Ministries with egg cartons, literally, that the Church secretary, Miss Drusilla Boddie, brought to me for arts and crafts.

At first, we could get no real money for the Ministry. The irony was that the more people and Church leaders attempted to hinder the Ministry, the more God the Holy Spirit blessed Youth Ministries to grow in radical new ways. One of our earliest bold steps was a gospel rap group with DeMark Thompson, Aaron Williams, Kevin Thompson, and Ivan Hicks. The rappers were cutting edge and innovative, in any church. That was where the youth were; and I went there. I took a risk that worked.

Before long, Metropolitan began to make large monetary and in-kind investment to support the students, faculty, and Garrison

School. We tithed the Tithe (10% of the gross amount of money the Church received) as a result of a Church-wide planning retreat. Garrison was one of our recipients. We gained the respect and attention of the Mayor, local elected officials, and the community. Dr. Joan Grant, who was the Director of the Migrant Farm Workers Program, which was housed at Garrison, and I became fast and close friends. Our direct service and financial contributions to Garrison, and the community, were most noteworthy. Iron sharpened iron.

As a servant, my goal was to make our Youth Ministries, and all the ministries, HUM. God did more than that. Every Saturday, from 9:00 a.m. till 3:00 p.m., we were on fire for the Lord. Children, teens, parents, and volunteers of all ages, The Hicks and the Millers were all present each week. Janet Thompson, who had DeMark and Sherica in Youth Ministries, and George C. Miller, Jr., who had our three children in Youth Ministries, were two of our strongest advocates; and they were members of the Board of Trustees. Their voices greatly helped us to move us forward with the financial backing of the Church.. The Presence of God inspired awe. WHEW!

One thing that continued to bother me more and more, daily, was the fact that drug houses and drug-addicted people surrounded Metropolitan. I couldn't reconcile that in my spirit that this darkness existed in the presence of our Church, and other Churches in our community. We had to take authority over the enemy, and rescue the people, in the Name of Jesus. Under the leadership of William Howard, Metropolitan had a very viable Alcoholics Anonymous Ministry that expanded to include the Narcotics Anonymous Ministry. God surely anointed Metropolitan Ministries in an unbelievable way; and placed them on the big screen. That view permitted me to see clearly, and extract all of the pictures that said things were out of line with the will of God concerning the darkness. Holiness and darkness could not dwell together.

In my mind, that contradiction of drug demons and our Church existing together did not line up with the will of God. The 7th Street corridor that was a part of our community was one of the worse drug corridors in the country, at the time. Shooting galleries for drug abuse were a prominent part of our landscape. I felt the overwhelming need to rescue the people from that life of addiction, and provide a safe environment for our Church family. God permitted me no rest regarding the matter.

One night, God gave me an incredible vision with instructions that made me most uncomfortable to convey. God said that the congregation was to leave the sanctuary after service, together, on a particular Sunday, and walk through the neighborhood in a certain direction that would cover several city blocks.

Needless to say, the vision and directions were so over-the-top that it was painful that some of our ministry staff, who were primarily volunteers, found the vision and instructions to be most humorous. To look ridiculous about something God says is not a good feeling. That feeling and those reactions would become an even more familiar part of my life for years to come, as they had already. That's the problem with receiving visions from God. The visionary has to transmit the vision to others who will likely neither see nor understand it, or desire to work to bring the vision to reality. The visionary is obligated to God to follow orders.

Though I loved the staff, and they came to respect me and the works God worked through me by then, love had nothing to do with their opposition. Pastor Hicks reached a compromise plan that we would walk half the distance that God told me we were to walk in the vision. We would walk the foursquare block surrounding the Church. I had to make the congregational announcement. We did that. After planning and organizing the logistics, which George led, over 1,200 people walked that Sunday after the 11:00 a.m. worship service. We followed a carefully designed strategic plan for exiting the building and marching. That victory march was an absolutely marvelous move of God. We could feel the power of God the Holy Spirit. Church family was exuberant, but reverent and strong. What a day that was.

On the Monday that followed the Joshua March, the unthinkable, the unbelievable happened. A man who owned some of the properties across the street came over to ask if Metropolitan wanted to buy the houses that he owned. In the following weeks, more of the owners of the houses that we marched pass came to offer their properties to Metropolitan for purchase. George and the Trustees rapidly pulled together a loan proposal, which was approved; and Metropolitan bought the properties.

At the same time, the neighborhood was changed; and the enrollment at the school dropped dramatically. Therefore, because of the work we did for the students and community, Mayor Marion Barry and the D.C. City Council offered the Garrison School building and play ground where we parked to the Metropolitan Baptist Church for at the price of one dollar ($1.00), for some prolonged period of time.). I am sure that God set up absolutely everything for our victory and success. Who expected those blessings? Over 30 years later, it is still difficult to understand why some members of the leadership declined the offer to occupy the land. That failure of faith would come back to brutally assault the Church. Even so, we give God the glory.

God the Holy Spirit did so many unbelievable things for us that I cannot tell all of the details. When those properties fell to us that was, without a shadow of doubt, a modern-day, Bible-based,

Jericho experience. The impenetrable walls came down. The mind of my spirit has often wondered what would have happened if we had walked the distance God told us to walk. Nevertheless, it was a marvelous, real-time, manifestation of the walls of Jericho tumbling down.

From that Miracle, God taught me even better how to follow the Biblical precedence and paradigm. That was only the beginning. Two years after I first started, the volunteer position became a full-time, salaried position. The full-time paid staff expanded in size, as we worked around the clock, almost. God added an average of 25 new members to our Metropolitan family each Sunday. We worked.

God the Holy Spirit moved in such amazing ways. I attempted to sing in the Young Adult Fellowship Ensemble. That did not pan out because of my mother duties. I could never make choir rehearsals. I bought the usher's uniform and served for a while on the Senior Ushers Ministry. George was the President, but we always had to coordinate our schedules so that one of us was always with the children. So, the Ushers Ministry did not work out too well for the same reason. I was on the Hospitality Committee for a while. That did not work out for the same reason. My inability to serve in other ministries was disappointing, but nothing came before my husband and our children. And, I would not substitute those ministries for what God called me to do as a wife and mother. I could not do that. In my head, I constantly reminded myself that we only had one chance to rear our sons and daughter correctly, as the children of God.

Pastor Hicks asked me to help plan the Annual Church-Wide Retreats. I had never organized a retreat before either. God led me to accept the role; and gave me all the people and knowledge that was needed to hold successful retreats. We took our children with us there and everywhere that we went through the years. I loved coordinating the retreats; and God gave the vision and revelation to format them.

God the Holy Spirit totally was all in our midst. The word retreat was changed to the Annual Church-Wide Summit. God moved us forward. Secretly, I hoped God was satisfied with my works, so I could avoid doing the next thing. George coordinated the Church-wide cookouts which came as a result of one of the Summits. The cookouts were phenomenal with upwards of 1,500-2,000 people who attended each year; and a battalion of incredibly fantastic volunteers who worked humbly and mightily to prepare for major feasting on free barbecue, all kinds of side dishes,, desserts and fun galore.

The truth is that I ran as far as I could go to avoid doing what God called me to do from childhood. I attest to the fact that God's call upon our lives is non-negotiable. There was nowhere else to run. There was nowhere else to hide. For years, I suggested all of the sermons to other preachers to preach that God would permit. Metropolitan Baptist Church operated like a spiritually well-oiled machine, or dynamic Church. God's vibrations grew louder.

All of us were pleased and blessed to play our part in the work of God the Holy Spirit. Somehow, the daily ministry that God orchestrated through my life made my call seem even more legitimate and urgent. A Pastor in Richmond, Virginia called me a "Bootlegger" because he said I was preaching without a license. That happened a lot when I thought I was just talking. He, like so many others, just spoke that out of the blue. Whenever that happened, we all laughed, but my conviction grew deeper. My disobedience felt enormously uncomfortable, with a greater desire in my spirit to get my calling right, to be in God's will.

Under the divine leadership of God the Holy Spirit, and the

Pastorate of Reverend Dr. H. Beecher Hicks, Jr., Metropolitan was a megachurch with 8,000 plus members, before megachurch was even a word. We were a seven-day-a-week Ministry. Our Church family would come for Bible Study, ministry meetings, or choir rehearsal each day; or come by the Church for no reason at all, just to hang out.

Metropolitan was an example of an astounding move of Almighty God, Who worked so many amazing wonders, in us, through us, and for us. At the same time, for me, pertaining to God's call on my life, Psalm 139 became an inescapable description of my existence. In a sense, the narrow path could no longer be navigated, the way I thought it could. Being trapped between the rock and the hard place became unbearable, as well. In this context, God persistently called me. Circumstances became such that I could no longer tolerate myself and my disobedience. I was repulsive to me.

God is love. God is patient. Love is patient. Twice, my husband was asked to be a Deacon. The first time he declined because he did not feel he was ready. In order for him to become a Deacon, I had to become a Deaconess as his wife. The consideration was an extreme honor for me to support my husband in any circumstance. Needless to say, I knew that the Deaconess Ministry, though highly honorable, was not my calling. In addition, the case that I put forward to the Pastor was that people, males and females, should be chosen to become Deacons based on their own Christian walk and individual merit, married or single. The person's spiritual walk as a Christian is the most important factor for the office; not that they are married to someone, as the tradition had been in the Baptist Church.

There was sufficient Biblical precedence in the Acts of the Apostles to put forth the case that women should be chosen as

Deacons, too. God made the Biblical facts clear and I presented the Greek etymology of the word Deacon. I remained on that soapbox. George was ordained a Deacon; and I was Consecrated a Deaconess. Pastor Hicks assigned him to the Trustee Ministry; and he became Vice Chairman. He helped to manage the Budget and Finance Committee; and performed an excellent service for the Church. God placed us neatly where God wanted us, and where we would do the most effective, good ministry works.

The additional blessing was that God put me on duty to learn all aspects of ministry to which access would have been denied otherwise. Chairwoman Georgia Whited gave me the awesome responsibility for Baptism. As staff and a member of the Christian Discipleship Council, I assisted with the New Members Training. The honor of these assignments was so great for me, that in a way, I felt as if I received Jesus Christ's sandals or something. Without saying a word, God moved me so close to the heavenly fire that I began to feel the radiant heat. Ha! God is God!

All of the assignments gave me priceless, on-the-job-training, that I did not have or expect... just like that. The opportunity for me to see, do the work, and add other very important dimensions of service to the Church experiences and to my ministry life was wondrously mind blowing.. Every preacher should be required to do similar on-the-job training in preparation for ministry. In my head, I really thought God was satisfied with all that I did. I knew better. The call still stood ever before me in bold relief. God completed the plan for everything before the foundation of the world. God does not change God's mind. We have, within our power, to answer yes to whatever God's plan entails.

The opportunity to organize the Baptism in a more excellent way was beyond thrilling. God made a way for us to purchase all new storage equipment; renovate closet space to store everything associated with Baptism and Holy Communion; and provided all new Baptism attire for the candidates. After all, we baptized an average of 25 or more people every month, especially during the height of major national events like Desert Storm. It is yet my firm belief that the Baptism and Holy Communion and everything pertaining to them merit the upmost respect and attentiveness. My staff position helped me to move the purchase of new attire and equipment forward for Baptism.

Neither time nor space will permit me to detail the blessings of our Victorious Christian Living Bible Class that I taught every Sunday after the 8:00 a.m. service. There were 500 people on the roll. At least three hundred showed up every Sunday. To teach that class literally gave me life; the fortitude to do everything else that God required; and the ability to win the fights against the enemy. We studied the Bible in the context of winning through Jesus Christ, the Anointed Messiah. Do not dare think the enemy did not oppose us from the beginning. He did. We won.

I still miss the members of that class. AND, though all of us have been blessed with other experiences of ministry, it is most unlikely that any of us, as many have told me, will have another experience that equals to that of the "Purple People" of Victorious Christian Living. Pastor Hicks always jokingly called us Miller Memorial Baptist Church. The power of God the Holy Spirit moved in us and through us. I truly see all that happened, now, as the way God already planned every detail. The memories of our class yet comfort me, like my purple shawl. God used me to teach an at least three other classes each session, and New Members Class.

God squeezed my response to God's call to preach out of me, bit by bit, drip by drip. Every Sunday, the sermons that Dr. Hicks preached slayed me in the Spirit. Did I mention that I was also a

Prayer Partner? I could barely do that job after the morning message was preached because I was spiritually wiped out. However, nothing was ever permitted to conflict with my first ministry as my husband's wife and our children's mother. That was well known. God systematically added the wood, and the fire of God the Holy Spirit grew hotter and hotter. God had me in an inescapable place with no way out.

Two very devastating things happened. Dr. Sergio Fabro was killed in a car accident in some foreign country. My childhood Pastor, Reverend Dr. Julius C. Williams, died from a massive heart attack, also. Reverend Williams always knew that I was a preacher; and imparted into my spirit for many years, from my pre-teen years through my young adult life. He approved of every message I was permitted to deliver for special Sundays during my teen years. Though Reverend and Mrs. Williams had no biological children, they touched thousands of lives as spiritual parents who led souls to salvation. The two people who helped me so significantly in the two most important areas of my life, faith and family, to that point, were suddenly no longer here on this earth. For the first time in my life, the feeling of abandonment became all too real, and there was no escape from that pit of anguish.

Dr. Fabro's Administrative Assistant was my wonderful friend. That morning, she called to tell me the news that Dr. Fabro was killed in some foreign country. That news struck a blow to my soul. The rest of the conversation was completely void of comprehension on my part. I literally dropped to the floor; and was deluged in agony and despair over the loss. I sat in his memorial service and listened to all of the marvelous, incredible, accolades that Dr. Fabro was given from his professional colleagues in medicine and academia. Such honor and more was rightly deserved. Yet, my heart and soul felt like they were ripped in pieces. For me, our family, and so many countless other women and their families, Dr. Fabro was also another person.

The urge to say something, to jump up and exclaim who Dr. Fabro was from the point of view of his patients, overwhelmed me. As I sobbed endlessly, it was as if they spoke of someone else, someone I never met. The need to talk about our prophetic physician demanded me to tell the phenomenal, august crowd who gathered in that serene setting our family's story with Dr. Fabro. The compulsion to say something drove me to be a spokesperson by proxy for the countless other women, fathers and families who were granted live births; and those who were not. Amazingly, unexpectedly, God granted fulfillment of my desire to speak. I was not on the program, but God changed the format right before me. The next thing I knew, I was on the pulpit; but I did not know how I got there.

There is no way I can describe how profound that change in the program was. In retrospect, I now feel like that was my first eulogy, though I brought remarks at Homegoings a few times before. Though I was heartbroken, there is no doubt in my mind that God orchestrated the allotted time for me to speak about the genuine genius of this man in medicine; and his time in the lives of mothers, fathers, and babies. I spoke for all the women like me, the fathers like George, and the thousands of children that he delivered. The seed will continue to reproduce. Generations yet unborn will live because God worked the impossible to create the possible through Dr. Fabro. I was immensely humbled and honored. For that grace, I had to be about my Heavenly Father's business. To remain in sorrow's valley was not permitted.

To write this book, I searched the Internet to see if there was any information about Dr. Fabro. The web didn't exist back then; and I would not have been brave enough to search for his name, even if it did exist. For the first time, I learned a little more about why he testified before the U.S. Congress panel that day when God led me to see him on the national evening news. Perhaps, the article also explains the expressions of amazement on some of the physicians' faces at the memorial service when our family's story was told that Dr. Fabro prescribed magnums of wine to save our baby. Nothing he did for me lined up with his research and his desperate decision. That is why Miracles are Miracles. Nothing ever lines up or computes as normal when a Miracle is in play.

You will forgive me for including the following short article. You will understand better why I did so, by-and-by. I took note of the fact that the article was written just three months before our first son was born on May 25, 1979. I was on the magnums of wine when the article was written. Irony of ironies, God used wine to save our son in the womb. The same thing that harmed other babies blessed us through the intervention of the Divine.

Despite the findings and the risk, Dr. Fabro prescribed a gallon of wine every day for months; but I was never drunk. No matter how many times over the years I go over this fact in my head intellectually, I can never make sense of the reality that I was never drunk. I am not a drinker. I should have been plastered. How it must have pained him to give me that prescription, knowing him. How it must have troubled him his research whose conclusion spoke of the potential danger.

(From the Herald Tribune - Feb. 10-11, 1979)
Drinking and Birth Defects Linked!
by Victor Cohn

(U.S.) FEDERAL OFFICIALS WARNED that even mild drinking during pregnancy may be a cause of birth defects. There is overwhelming evidence said Dr. Judith Hall, a Seattle medical geneticist, that heavy

drinking causes a severe "fetal alcohol syndrome" in one newborn in every 2,000 in the United States. Although firm evidence is lacking, she said, even light drinking probably causes adverse effects in as many as one or two infants in 1,000.

These could include still-births and lower birth weight, as well as, hyperactivity and behavioral effects, according to some research. Dr. Sergio Fabro, head of fetal-maternal medicine at George Washington University, agreed that heavy drinking may cause problems in the central nervous system that could produce mental retardation & a "cluster" of facial abnormalities.

OF LIGHTER DRINKING, he said only that "some toxicity suspicious of or compatible with alcohol toxicity has been observed" after consumption of an ounce of pure alcohol daily-the amount in two ounces of 100-proof liquor or two four- ounce glasses of wine. "As an intelligent guess," he said, "substantial and serious risk" may begin when a woman drinks three or more ounces of pure alcohol, about three stiff drinks daily.

1 Corinthians 1:27-28 – "But God hath chosen the foolish things of the world to confound the wise; and God hath chosen the weak things of the world to confound the things that are mighty; And base things of the world, and things which are despised, hath God chosen, yea, and things which are not, to bring to naught things that are:"

God the Holy Spirit works through people in all of the experiences of life. Reverend Dr. Julius C. Williams and Dr. Sergio Fabro lived out their God-Given assignments to the fullest. They served Almighty God through outstanding service to people. They were humble and generous, without consideration of themselves. One walks away from an encounter with people like them knowing that God assigned us to meet and journey together, for however long that journey lasts here on earth. One gets a sense that God reserved a special place in heaven just for them and their wives. Neither couple had children. They surely made the way for others to bring children in the world to serve God. All I can think about is how gracious is our God that God permitted me to know these mighty and generous souls.

Musings with God the Holy Spirit!

- So vast is the will of God that the human mind is without faculties to understand the will's inherent qualities.
- Sometimes, we wonder why God did what was done. In those instances, I have but one conclusion: God is God, alone. Let it be.
- Everything God does is for God's glory and our best good.
- Proverbs 3:5 – "Trust in the Lord with all thine heart; and lean not unto thine own understanding. In all thy ways acknowledge him, and He shall direct thy paths."
- If we are going to do the will of God, God's way, we have to acknowledge the confounding things that are sometimes a part of God's modus operandi (MO).
- Like Miracles, confounding things are intended to cause us to look at God for revelations; and to give God glory before and after the outcome, whatever that outcome is.
- Confounding things should cause us to confess to God that we cannot do what is required without God.
- God the Holy Spirit empowers us to do the will of God in ways that are beyond our human ability or thought capacity.
- Conditions for God to work God's plan are not dependent upon the circumstances of humans or nature.
- God is Creator of all good things.

- God currently knows the will, whereabouts, and everything pertaining to humans, from the first Adam then Eve, to the last of all creation.
- No Adam or Eve is dead.
- Every Adam and every Eve, every woman, man, boy, and girl is either alive in heaven; or alive in the earth; or alive in hell.
- We get to decide where we will spend eternity.
- Only good comes from God; and never evil.
- Maintain an expectant hope, no matter what.
- Faith in God unveils what is real and good.
- God's reality and our understanding of that reality are often two different things.
- God is correct.
- God is strong.
- God is Holy.
- God is Perfection.
- God is Absolute.
- We thank GOD for our afflictions and infirmities because some of Christ's power, "dunamis", is transferred to us through our endurance.
- Through our obedience to God, God grants us unlimited access to God's "dunamis".
- As the daughters and sons of God, because of Jesus Christ, we have access to power equivalent to dynamite within us.
- 2 Samuel 22:33 – "God is my strength and power: and he maketh my way perfect."
- 2 Corinthians 12:9 – "And he said unto me, My grace is sufficient for thee: for my strength is made perfect in weakness. Most gladly therefore will I rather glory in my infirmities, that the power of Christ may rest upon me."
- Thank God for Grace.
- When we obediently submit to God, the power of God washes over us.
- Humbly receive the knowledge and power of God.

97

Chapter 8
Oh God!
The Process Processes ME!

Jeremiah 1:5 - "Before I formed thee in the belly I knew thee, and before thou camest forth out of the womb I sanctified thee, and I ordained thee a prophet unto the nations."

I am fully persuaded and have often conveyed to others that if there is no struggle to accept the call to preach, there is probably no call from God. When the preacher accepts the call to preach the gospel, the feeling of unworthiness and trepidation are mind boggling. We lose friends and gain enemies, immediately. That makes the reality of the struggle even more pronounced, but a ready sign, one indicator, that the call is real.

Preaching can never be an escape from something or someone else; or an excuse "to preach" because other things didn't work out. I saw and yet see a great deal of that. Jesus said that many have gone out in His Name, but He did not call them or send them. That thought, as even a remote possibility, horrified me. All of my life, my desire has been that God would use me; and be pleased with my work as a Christian. God's will is that we obey God. Our call is God's decision to use us to help God the Holy Spirit create an environment and opportunity for salvation through Jesus Christ; and good works as a result of our faith..

Our best teacher is God the Holy Spirit who demonstrates through creation the amazing wonders of truth. "Metamorphoo" is the Greek word for change that God the Holy Spirit presses me to raise here. The **New Testament Greek Lexicon** defines metamorphoo as a change in form that includes transformation and transfiguration. Needless to say, change is required for all of creation. Change happens whether we know it or not; or whether we like it or not. The most obvious of God's creations to display "metamorphoo" as transformation is the butterfly.

My passion for butterflies is well known among certain people. One day God gave me a special treat through God's grace. There was a caterpillar clinging to the outside wall of our home. I felt sad that it was so far away from the grass, but I was led to leave it alone and not toss it out into the yard. God the Holy Spirit had arranged a powerful lesson without my knowledge.

The next day, I saw this hideous looking glob. I forgot about the caterpillar from the day before; and did not consider at all the scientific morphing process. I just decided that I would leave the yucky stuff there for someone else to clean off for me. However, at that moment, though I was somewhat grossed out, God led me to take a closer look. Upon closer inspection, I could see all of my favorite colors – purple, yellow, green, blue, and black – in a beautiful display. The colors were fantastic with an amazing sheen to them. Still, I did not get it, though I was amazed at what I saw. To remember what was not correctly processed, in my mind, would be a powerful lesson.

The following day, God led me back outside to take a look. The glob was gone without a trace. There was absolutely no evidence that it was ever on the wall. I just assumed my husband cleaned it off. Great, I thought. It's gone. Well, not exactly. I went to the front yard to get the mail and there it was. The transformed glob became the most incredibly beautiful butterfly with all the colors I saw in the yucky form; and lines and circles were perfectly placed. God stationed that magnificent creation right where I could see it; then convinced me to go outside at just the right moment. The butterfly just sat there, waiting I suppose to embrace the transformation that the morphing caused. The Holy Spirit let me know, in fact, that God did that just for me. So, I thanked God for its exquisite beauty. I told the butterfly to enjoy the journey and thanks for enduring the process of transformation for all who would behold its beauty, including me. Gently, it flew away.

Morphing changes not just the form, but also the substance of that which is morphed, even though we cannot see the change. Like that butterfly, God let me know, for the purpose of this book, that the morphing or changes that I experienced were a part of a process to become a real preacher. Through God's process of morphing me into a preacher, I realized that one of the great difficulties in my life that I had to resolve over the course of my lifetime was that God called me to preach the gospel before I was born. I did not fully grasp that truth until I really sat with Jeremiah 1:5, many times. My experience does not reflect a single occasion, but years of "calling". Like the story recorded in I Samuel 3:10 regarding the prophet, my own story is very similar. Even now, the memories of the callings flood my spirit.

The "Voice" began calling me when I was around five or six years old, and continued for years afterwards. I heard my name actually called in the most unusual situations, sometimes with no one around. I heard the "Voice" call me when I walked home from school, which should have made me crazy. There were times that I heard the "Voice" call my name when I studied alone; played in the yard; or sang in choir rehearsal as a kid. There was no way to predict when or where the intrusion would enter. The "Voice" called my name in the classroom, as the teacher taught; in the car or on the bus; or at home, even in the midst of the noise of five children, three adults and a dog or whoever else might be there for dinner, at the time; or, in total silence while we slept. The most disarming times were when I heard my name on the wind.

Though I have received criticism about my desire to always please our parents, even from a Seminary professor, I always wanted to obey that Fifth Commandment. My Mother, Father, and Grandmother were everything to me. I ran to them for years to respond to what I thought was their summons. They always answered, "No, I didn't call you". They called me a lot to do so many things. Hmmm! I convinced myself that I was just imagining things. I grew to despise my first name, and the day that name was ever given to me. I convinced myself that the name Nawanna sounded like so many other words that I thought people called me when they did not. Like an abused person, I blamed myself for hearing incorrectly. The thought also crossed my mind for years that something was wrong with me. Even now, I still have a little flutter whenever others speak my name aloud for any reason because of those experiences. I preferred my nickname. The parents did not because of slavery and jim crow. (I will not capitalize that name because of the atrocities.)

When I was around eleven or twelve years old, I told Mimi, my maternal Grandmother about the experiences of hearing my name called. Mimi lived with us and was always attentive to us. She told me that if I ever heard my name called like that again, do not answer. The gravity in her face and voice convinced me to do as I was told. Through the years, and even now, I attempted to figure out why Mimi told me that. She was a devout Christian, so I figured she knew something I did not know.

At first, I thought it was because Grandmama believed the "Voice" was some ghost from the dead that summoned me; and I would die if I answered again. More frequently, through the years, I came to believe that she knew God called me. But what was a woman to do with such a call, if she answered? Maybe, but most unlikely, she didn't know at all what the calling of my name was about. At all costs, she just wanted to protect me against whatever that was. I am grateful, whatever her motive was. At least my Grandmother believed me, and so I didn't tell anyone else, until now. Either way, I never answered "that Voice" again. Eventually, I also knew the "Voice" was God. I just hoped I was mistaken. Even now, I sound a little loony, right?

However, a different method or a new form of contact came about as an urging in my soul. As a result of those urgings, I really wanted to be a nun, even more than I did at age five or six, but we still were not Catholic. We were A.M.E. I also wanted to be a foreign missionary. I considered for a long time being a preacher, to myself; but I concluded God would have chosen me to be a foreign missionary instead. Yet, on those occasions when Reverend Williams asked me to speak for the Youth Day Services, I was both exhilarated and petrified. People in attendance always made a really big deal about the speeches I wrote and delivered.

Needless to say, I took the long way through the wilderness of rebellion against preaching. I followed God's commands in everything else, but just not answering God's call. Besides, I was too young to do much of anything but study, learn, and follow adult's orders. The prophet Samuel had similar issues with which I could identify. That wilderness in which I was stuck was my own creation. The way out is always there, even as there was an exit for the Israelites out of their wilderness. Just obey! I didn't. I spent years attempting to figure out and negotiate my options with God. God already stamped non-negotiable on our lives and assignment.. Jesus already paid the price for who God called us to be. Choosing anything but the way God chose for us is dangerous.

Then, one day, the urging also stopped. I didn't hear God call my name, anymore as in the past; and I did not feel the urge of the calling. I really hoped all of that was over for good. However, God never stopped drawing me through dreams and visions. God's Divine Presence paid me many visits – the same Presence I saw in that high chair and sensed throughout my life. Miracle upon Miracle urged me on, most especially the Miraculous birth of our three children. Each successive Miracle was more dramatic than the last. They were not just the ones God did in my own life, but those that God worked through me in the lives of other people. I never let them distract me. The impact of years and years of dreams, visions and hearing God call my name can't be calculated. With each successive dream or vision, more and more of the natural me drained out. That was a good thing, but I didn't know that, either. I knew God saved me for something. To be honest, I knew what the something was. Signs for me to do something other than preach were those indicators for which I looked and hoped. They were not there. Preaching was.

The last two dreams that almost spiritually and emotionally devoured me placed me squarely between the rock and the hard place. Conversations between God and me were silenced. God said nothing to me. All I could think of was the 430-450 years between the Old Testament and the New Testament when God was silent. The feeling of being lost without God was real. I got the message. God was finished speaking on the subject. In my spirit, I knew God was still there, but would not speak to me. What a dreadful feeling was given in place of God's voice.

The dreams were God's only communication; and I didn't like that. To shudder with your thoughts in silence and what seemed like God's abandonment is no joke. Who can really help you? Disobedience can cause self-imposed isolation from God; and shame before God, and others. All of my life, people told me that they believed I was called me to preach. I kept those thoughts at a distance. Confirmation of others for your call is a part of the process. I just didn't want to hear people say that any more, or give my lofty explanation of why that was not true. It is written:

Matthew 24:16-18 – " Then let them which be in Judaea flee into the mountains: Let him which is on the housetop not come down to take anything out of his house: Neither let him which is in the field return back to take his clothes."

Different versions of a repetitive dream that haunted me were based on Matthew 24:16-18. The words of those texts just floated out of the spirit of living waters. They presented themselves like a screenplay, filled with light, action, sounds, smells, and horrors. In one of the dreams, everything in my Fairfax neighborhood was on fire. I told people to run to the west, towards the mountains in Virginia, though they were far away. Unlike the housetop roofs of that day when this scripture was written, people attempted to climb up on their modern day roofs, but slid down. It seemed that no matter where the people were, God instructed me to tell them what they should do based on those texts. Those final series of dreams in particular grieved me, enormously. Our home and my family were always safe, but that didn't stop my compulsion to speak to the people about how to flee to safety through the Salvation of Jesus Christ.

God's silence and the dreams definitely drove me to the next place. There were a few more rounds of mortal combat that would begin the death of the layperson that I was in order that the preacher might be born. In a sense, a very spiritually real sense, I was pregnant with the preacher that God called, before the foundation of the world. I wrestled with the question that I knew would be asked. Because of family obligations, it was impossible to go away to a retreat alone. Everything played out in the course of daily life and responsibilities to my husband, children, and work. Like Jacob, the wrestling with God was personal, private and best for me, but that is not the only way. Like Mary, one must ponder with God in the heart. God has all the answers, love and patience that are needed.

I knew I must ultimately answer, publicly, during the Ordination this question: "What is the experience of your call?" For years, I didn't think I had a specific experience, date and time like other preachers told me that they had. Therefore, I justified in my own head that apparently God did not call me since I couldn't remember the experience. That was a weak excuse; but all of my excuses were weak. The other question that I knew would be a part of the public Catechism for which I had no answer was what was my experience of rebirth? Every preacher I ever heard had specifics about their conversion. I didn't. Surely, if I had one, I would remember! God would have told me, right?

Out of nowhere, God matter-of-factly moved me through my self-imposed wilderness. One day, while at work, as I walked through the sanctuary, as I often did, to get to the administration building, I heard God speak. "John the Baptist", God said. O WOW! Oh, my LORD. God spoke to me, again. I couldn't believe it. I wanted to somehow hug God with all my might because I was so elated. That was it. That was all that God said. It had been so long since I heard God speak, a most uncomfortable dry spell in my life. I knew without a shadow of doubt that God was with me, just silent. A bit startled, I sat down on the front row. and pulled a Bible from the rack behind me.

I reread Luke 1:15. Instantaneously, I knew that was the answer. I read that passage many times before. Why didn't I get it before? Finally, I received "and he (John the Baptist) shall be filled with the Holy Ghost, even from his mother's womb." When the Lord led me to combine the experience of Samuel's call with the birth of John the Baptist, the floodgates of the Spirit opened full-force. Tears streamed down my face. I held my breath in a protracted gasp for what seemed like hours. I was free. God let me know that was my story. Jeremiah 1:5 finally made sense. I was created for the call from the womb. God the Holy Spirit manifested in my life from the womb. How small and narrow are the ways that we assign to God based on how we interpret the power of God.

I finally knew that when I saw Jesus for the first time when I was in that high chair, it was not a fluke. I saw that same Jesus that day in the sanctuary. The Messiah met me, once more, at the point of my greatest need. Jesus was there with me, present, like He was in my infancy. Really, I was in infancy again – about to be birthed as a preacher. My overwhelming need was to know when did God call me and when did God convert me. I received my answers. Both occurred in the same hour. Like Jacob in Genesis 32:24-30, the wrestling with God was over. Like Jacob, that was my Peniel experience in the sanctuary, where I knew God; and sensed God face to face. Though I could not see God, God blessed me to know God's presence. I did not want to talk, or breathe, or think. And for the moment, God the Holy Spirit permitted me the genuine silence that wraps you in complete serenity. OH GOD!

In the silence, I realized that there were conversations that needed to be held with God, my husband, our children, and our Pastor – in that order. A long list of other people followed them; most significant among them were my Mama and Daddy. The most poignant statement came from my husband, as he attempted to process what all of this would mean to him and our family. He said, "But, I didn't marry a preacher." Did he or didn't he? In many ways, he was right. He did not. I was always hoping that the call would go away and it would not matter. God's call never went away. With a contrite spirit, I apologized to him for any actions that caused pain, difficulty, or uncertainty..

The challenges are many that arise when the call is finally accepted. If one who is called to the gospel ministry is married, female or male, there is a domino effect upon the family to which everyone is unwittingly subjected. That effect must be handled, meticulously, and intentionally, and upfront, if the individual family members are to embrace the call, too. They were. The enemy waits for a way to enter the family line and affect it for generations or destroy it completely. Take the time to talk everything through, regardless. The dialogue makes the steps easier for everyone to walk out God's assignment. In the days ahead, the family strives together for the perfecting of each family member, in the work of the ministry.

When we accept God's call to preach, everything changes, including relationships. Things change even more when the Ordination occurs. As I said, the preacher's lot is that she or he will instantly and progressively lose friends and gain enemies. Unlike any other profession, perhaps, the acceptance of the call to preach impacts others in your circle more than we thought. One of the critical indicators for me was that if God called me, God would make the call right for my family.

I just didn't believe that God would permit my acceptance of God's will to destroy the people who I loved the most – my husband and our children. I too had an obligation to consider them in every aspect. Proverbs 16:7 is abundantly true. My family was not and is not my enemy. The family unit must be managed in a Godly way, at all times. The real enemy seeks to establish a foothold to destroy marriages and the family. The marriage and family must be prayerfully guarded.

More specifically, as a female, I felt that nothing about my role as a wife and mother could go unattended, from the beginning, in general, period. God gave me the notion in my head that I could not and would not go out and preach and teach others and neglect my duties as a wife and mother at home. So, every day, I worked those works first – at home. I'm not sure that preachers who are male feel the same way. However, I believe the principle is valid for anyone who accepts the call to preach who has a family. The following scripture became even more significant. It is written:

Proverbs 16:7 – "When a man's ways please the Lord, he maketh even his enemies to be at peace with him."

George and our children were not my enemies. They were and are my greatly endeared and beloved heart; strongest supporters; counselors; and critics. Therefore, they deserved what I requested God to do for them and to give them. I determined that I would never blame anything on the call, as an excuse not to be who I agreed to be to our family, as a wife and mother. The misuse of the call is a preacher's poor excuse to mask the egotism that satan often perpetrates through preachers. We should not be wed to the call in ways that are spiritually and emotionally detrimental to ourselves or others. Our God-given assignment does not prevent us from being in relationship with family and people. God the Holy Spirit gives life through family, too, biological and spiritual.

Through the power of God the Holy Spirit, the determination was made that people would not be permitted to make our children "preacher's kids", as some people do in the Church. Then those same people turn around and talk about the children of preachers in ungodly ways. Not only was the role of a preacher who is Baptist and female new and challenging for me, it was equally challenging to be the husband and the children of a preacher who is female and Baptist. Long before accepting God's assignment for my life, I declared one thing. "My first ministry is to my husband, and our children." With God's help, it became clear that my movement through that declaration of preacher would be very strategic. There was no way that the enemy was gaining a foothold in our family. Our family structure cost.

The due diligence of the call and the acceptance proved to be what I call the "there-ness" of God about which Psalm 139 speaks. There is no place in the entire universe – heaven or hell – where it is possible to escape the presence, power and providence of God. God is there, wherever "there" is. Nevertheless, that fact did not prevent my futile attempt to escape God's eye and reach. The due diligence leads to the understanding that if God calls you, the burning flames within are set ablaze from mere embers of the Word of God that permeate the entire spirit and soul. Indeed, my testimony was, is and evermore shall be that of Jeremiah, "the weeping prophet". It is written:

Jeremiah 20:9 – "Then I said, I will not make mention of him, nor speak any more in his name. But his word was in mine heart as a burning fire shut up in my bones, and I was weary with forbearing, and I could not stay."

When God calls us, no matter what that call is, the summons to appear before God for service is inescapable. That call is irreversible. We may never accept God's call or do God's will, but God does not cancel either one. It is written:

Romans 11:29 - "For the gifts and calling **of** God are without repentance."

The Message Bible interprets that passage this way, "God's gifts and God's call are under full warranty – never cancelled, never rescinded". We are therefore compelled through due diligence to discern the call; and use the Gifts of God the Holy Spirit through the power of God the Holy Spirit to accept that to which God assigns us and what God says.

The due diligence revealed to me that if God removed everything and everyone from the preacher/prophet, the call is inextricably linked to the fabric of our identity. If God gave everything of a material nature to the preacher/prophet, whatever is received pales in the light of God's Word within the spirit of the preacher/prophet; and the Gifts of God the Holy Spirit who performs the works through us.

Therefore, to what extremes could one journey where God's call would cease to be that haunting presence? In my experience, there was no place on earth, or in heaven, or in hell like the Psalmist so eloquently postulated that one can escape. In fact, the very idea that one must preach with God, alone, is a part of the destination where the preacher must ultimately arrive through the process of due diligence. To arrive at the appointed assignment to become a preacher engages us in the struggle. The struggle includes the searching; the denying; the running; the hiding; the down-sitting; and the mounting up on wings of eagles. Struggle is a portion of the "wait on the Lord" that Isaiah 40:28-31 describes.

I went to talk to Pastor Hicks and to confess my call to preach. On Mother's Day, May 14, 1989, one day before my 38th birthday, I was scheduled to make my public confession of the call to preach before the congregation at the 8:00 a.m. service. On the way out of the door at home in the early morning hours, God led me to grab something, but I didn't know what that something was. A necklace that our daughter made in school was the object to which my attention was led. How odd was that direction, yet there was no time to ponder the instruction. Obey.

Basically, the necklace was a blue rope with five smooth stones on it that were made of plaster of Paris. A knot between the stones held them in place. Shortly, a thousand memories flooded my mind, as I held onto the necklace during the service. Daunting was the moment that had taken a lifetime to finally occur – the fullness of time. Over 50 people came to give their lives to Christ and unite with the Church that day. We were still in some major move of God, so that number was not uncommon. I did my duties, all the while I figured I had one last chance to escape the call – simply avoid the confession of it.

As soon as the Prayer Partners started to make the introductions of the new members, I very calmly got up and moved from my spot as a Deaconess. I swiftly shifted into my staff roll like I was going to do something very important that just came up. With the different roles that I performed on Sunday, that was not uncommon. Quickly the move was made toward the exit. The usher very graciously opened the door for me. As soon as I turned the corner, out of sight, I made a mad dash, sprinting around the back of the sanctuary hall in six-inch heels.

Where I was going, I still don't know. I just had to get out of there, out of the sanctuary, as quickly and non-disruptively as possible. When I made it to the exit on the other side, I ran smack-dab into the Chairman of the Board of Deacons, Odean Horne. Without either of us saying a word, I knew he knew. Deacon Horne looked at me with that look that a loving father gives when we are caught dead wrong in some unacceptable behavior. He said in a stern, fatherly voice, "Just where you think you are going young lady? March your little self right back in there."

I can still hear the sound of those words. The sound was like the loving though emphatic Voice of God, that turned me around. Feeling like I was a misbehaved kid, I did as I was told; but I felt very childlike and very tiny. No doubt, God orchestrated the interception because it was so perfect. I loved Deacon and Deaconess Horne. They were our spiritual parents along with Deacon and Deaconess Paige; Deacon and Deaconess O'Neal;

Deacon and Deaconess Branson; and so many more. Clearly, I was defeated. Or was I? God's people were on the scene.

Shortly, after I went back in the service, it was time, or should I say time was up. Clutching the necklace in my hands, I mounted the lower right pulpit to face nearly 1,500 people in the sanctuary, and those in two packed overflow sections who watched the service via television. Everything imaginable changed in that moment. Suddenly, peace overshadowed every objection of the enemy that I entertained. I looked into the faces of my husband, sons and daughter and realized that only God knew what was ahead for us. Only God knew that to which God called me. I made the confession of my call to preach based on the five smooth stones. In that moment, the necklace was the only source of strength available. They represented the stones that David picked up from the brook to go meet Goliath, the Philistine. The time had come to slay my spiritual Goliath. It is written:

Samuel 17:40 – "And he (David) took his staff in his hand, and chose him five smooth stones out of the brook, and put them in a shepherd's bag which he had, even in a scrip; and his sling was in his hand: and he drew near the Philistine."

Indeed, God slayed that spiritual Goliath for me who taunted me for so many years. That Goliath, for me, displayed my feeling of unworthiness to accept the call; and the feeling of inadequacy to accept the assignment. A simple necklace became God's tool to accomplish God's will. Goliath is anything or anyone that hinders the flow of God's plan for, in us, or through us. Here is the thing I didn't learn until later. "Giants just keep on coming", as I heard Dr. Hicks preach once. That truth is recorded in 2 Samuel 21:15-22. Goliath represents that looming, intimidating image. The

112

blessing is that once God uses us to slay that first giant, Goliath, we realize the enormous power of God who works on our behalf. Giants may keep coming, but we are stronger because of what God permitted us to overcome already.

Giants, both physical and spiritual, are slain with the power of God the Holy Spirit that comes upon a rock or anything else God places in our hands to use for that purpose. Even a string of five plaster of Paris rocks that a kid made are instruments for God to use. David had five smooth stones to kill Goliath. Why were there exactly five smooth rocks on that necklace that our daughter made, in her school, not Sunday school? God is always the only one in my details.

Faith permits that ridiculous thing that God gives us to take the giant out. We glorify God when we stand in faith; and that slain giant becomes our testimony to others to encourage them. Giants, in whatever form they assume, are there to oppose those who God calls and chooses. However, God's plan for our victory already incorporates the demise of the giants. If God permits the giants, God has provided the means to destroy the giants. Believe. We armor ourselves up with the Word of God and prayer. Show up. It's not our fight. The fight is God's fight.

The enemy ALWAYS opposes those who are called to do the will of God. The spirit of the Philistine is a spirit of opposition, and it is yet alive and active in all the earth to oppose God's sons and daughters. Nothing and no one can oppose God because God is God. So, satan opposes God's daughters and sons because of God's love for them. It is written:

Revelation 12:10 – "And I heard a loud voice saying in heaven, Now is come salvation, and strength, and the kingdom of our God, and the power **of** his Christ: for the accuser **of** our brethren is cast down, which accused them before our God day and night."

The accuser, no matter what form is assumed, is no match for God. David believed God. So did I. So do I. So will I. I wonder how many times did the accuser, satan, go to heaven to attempt to discredit me before God on just that one thing – God's call on my life to preach? I wonder how busy did I keep my angels who are assigned to me to protect me and engage me in thought to pursue my ministry assignment? As Christians, we are comforted to know and believe that God is in charge of our details. God works with us to bring God's plan into action. During God the Holy Spirit's process of processing me, I learned so much about God and myself. God restored me, despite my years of self-inflicted wounds. Yes! God dealt so wondrously with me that only the tracks of my tears testify. It is written:

Joel 2:25-26 – "I will restore to you the years that the locust hath eaten, the cankerworm, and the caterpillar, and the palmerworm, my great army which I sent among you. And ye shall eat in plenty, and be satisfied, and praise the name of the Lord your God that hath dealt wondrously with you: and my people shall never be ashamed."

Hallelujah! Over the years, those scriptures taught me such an enormous lesson concerning the grace, mercy, and deliverance of God. Like Israel, I was disobedient. Yet, God not only restores us, God fast-forwards us. God gave me knowledge and wisdom that could only have come from God about ministry. It would have taken years of experience as a preacher to get what God gave me, every time I was given an assignment. What God taught me was that if we operate in faith, God will teach us and process us to perform the works to which God called and assigned us. I never knew how to do anything that God led or told me to do. But, like God's call to Peter to walk on the water, we have to get out of the boat; keep our eyes on Christ; and move forward in Christ, towards Christ. It is written:

Proverbs 18:16 - "A man's gift maketh room for him, and bringeth him before great men."

To me the great men and women were those who remained open to the will of God without futilely attempting to inject or project their opinions on God. Despite the naysayers and their disparaging thoughts and attitudes, and opinions back then and even now about preachers who are female, Joel 2:25-26 and Proverbs 18:16 are phenomenal truths in my life. God restored the years that I thought were lost through my years of disobedience. They are the balm that heal my self-inflicted wounds.

In many regards, God placed me in coveted ministry positions and fast forwarded my progression as a preacher. Believe the Word of God. Just do what God says, quickly. No matter how many people already do what God calls you to do, decide to do that thing to the best of your God-given abilities. God lays out your call in such a way that even the enemy knows the powerlessness of his/her work against it.

From experience, I can tell you that there is boundless beauty in letting go of any and all preconceived notions about the call to preach or any other call. Far better are the hours expended to watch the unfurling of God's Grace, and the assignment of God's work in us and through us. We become available to receive priceless treasures of inconceivable knowledge and wisdom that we could never obtain otherwise. God rewards obedience. God is fully invested in us through Jesus Christ who paid it all. God's will is for us to represent Christ and His Kingdom. Faith in God's will alone is not a substitute for hard work.

Sometimes, the tendency is to lapse into the ordinary, when, in fact we are recreated to be powerfully exceptional. Through Jesus Christ, and the acts of Salvation that Jesus endured for us, all necessary acts of Divine Love are completed for our victory.

<u>Musings with God the Holy Spirit!</u>

- God knows and sees all.
- Ask God the Holy Spirit to guide you into all Truth.
- Never permit your God-given abilities to be displaced or measured against the attributes of someone else.
- God rewards obedience.
- God requires obedience.
- There is a distinct difference between obedience to the Will of Almighty God and ceremonies of convenience.
- I Samuel 15:22 – "And Samuel said, Hath the Lord as great delight in burnt offerings and sacrifices, as in obeying the voice of the Lord? Behold, to obey is better than sacrifice, and to hearken than the fat of rams."
- Listen and obey the Voice of God.
- Matthew 5:13-14 – "Ye are the salt of the earth… Ye are the light of the world…"
- Be the salt.
- Be the light.
- Be the city, on the hill, in full view and full power.
- Live in full view of the Master.
- Compromise is unacceptable.

Chapter 9
Oh God!
Due Diligence Confirmed Your Call!

2 Peter 1:10-12 – "Therefore, brethren, be even more diligent to make your call and election sure, for if you do these things you will never stumble; for so an entrance will be supplied to you abundantly into the everlasting kingdom of our Lord and Savior Jesus Christ. For this reason I will not be negligent to remind you always of these things, though you know them and are established in the present truth."

Alas, finally, I confessed my lifelong call to preach the Gospel. Deacon Horne made the motion that the Metropolitan Baptist Church grant me the opportunity to preach my initial sermon. Multiple Deacons, including the Vice Chairman Lawrence Paige and Deacon Maurice O'Neal seconded the motion. These righteous men were my spiritual fathers who honored God and blessed me beyond comparison. Even people in the congregation shouted out seconds to the motion. It was hilarious, as Pastor Hicks attempted to restore order; and pointed out that only the Deacons were qualified to second the motion. The motion was unanimously affirmed to thunderous applause, and a standing ovation from the congregation. The date was set for the initial sermon, also to be held during the 8:00 a.m. worship. God the Holy Spirit honored the motion and prepared the way.

Is the promise true in 2 Peter 1:10-12 that if I did the necessary due-diligence to provide surety for my call that I would not stumble? Yes! Thank God the promise is true! The Word of God is eternally true, "without mixture of error", in any of its dimensions. Did I stumble in other ways? Yes! Those were the times of God's on-the-job training when I did not follow God's directions given through the due-diligence before I took the next step. Those were the times through which God worked out my deficiencies. Even our mistakes are useful in God's hands. God already incorporated them in the plan.

Through the years, I had a thousand excuses for why God could not possibly be calling me to preach. I could eloquently and elaborately justify each excuse in my own mind, and to others who kept saying God called me to be a preacher. I never liked hearing that. Yet, God gave thousands of revelations why to preach was God's will for me. Two things, recurring dreams and a conversation with Pastor Hicks, pushed me beyond the point of resistance and refusal. I like to think I never denied the call; but what I did was still blatantly disobedient.

There was and still is one dream that drove me to the brink, and yet overwhelms me. Press play in my head and the drama begins as if it is a brand new movie. The impact of that dream drives me every day, so I will replay it in the present tense. The dream acts as my constant chastening rod not to buckle when people say God did not call "a woman" to preach.

In this dream, I am on the top of a very high mountain somewhere in Africa. Amazingly rich and melodiously beautiful singing that comes from the base of the mountain permeates the air. The sound of the singing is incredible, better than any singing I have ever heard. When I go over to the edge of a ridge to see from where the singing is coming, the sides of the mountain are covered with people. The people are staggered at all levels. They are arrayed in magnificently colored garments of rich hues whose beauty matches the sounds of their voices. I cannot understand the language that seems to be many languages, and yet one; but I know they praise God. Even with many languages, the voices merged as if only one language is spoken. I keep my eyes on them as I spoke to the Presence of God. I ask God what the scene and the people mean. Who are all these people?

God and I communicate without words, as we did when I had the out-of-body experience during the birth of our daughter. Spirit to spirit, no words, God says, "These are the people to whom I send you". That is it. That is enough. As I descend the mountain, God's presence covers it, as countless hands reach out to me in pain that expresses need that I can help to fulfill. I know the people, though I have never met them.

But, why did God choose Africa? Why did God choose these people? Over and over again, the last part of that same dream played out in short form, even in awake states, as though it was on continuous loop; and it interrupted my thoughts at will. I just knew in my soul what I had to do. How was the never-ending question? "HOW" is God's business. Forever, I would know that those who are given the assignment from God to preach the Gospel cannot stay on the mountain in some euphoric state of holiness. We must go to the valley to embrace the people, and lead people to Christ – the Rock - Who meets their need. We must help God to break yokes; and show people how to live the Christ-life, and live it more abundantly. Jesus is Lord and the spiritual Mountain of Truth like Mt. Gerizim of Deuteronomy 27:12 from whom Truth flows to all who believe.

The mind and soul of the preacher will always remember the question that Pastor Hicks asked me because the question and my response were so critical to my life. He said, "Could you live the rest of your life and never preach a Word in His Name?" The answer was a heart rending, tearful no. I could not bear the thought.

Finally! The line was crossed once the call on my life was confessed before the Church. **I reached vertigo, the point of no return, a sermon subject that I delivered early in my preaching ministry. As pilots say, I reached vertigo – the point of no return. I must go forward.** The new walk was ground zero for the "would-be preacher". The next day after the confession, the challenge to walk in the calling began. I learned that the one who God calls is not suddenly a preacher. Preaching is another level of commitment to God that requires even more subjection to God, and study with God the Holy Spirit.. To become a preacher is indeed a rather slow morphing process rather than some meteoric rise to the top. That understanding is severely lacking in the current ministry trend of the 21st century. Even the Apostle Paul went away, off the scene, for three years when he accepted God's call. Jesus let Paul be knocked of the donkey and blinded so Paul would see. Submit to the God the Holy Spirit Who will teach you..

The new walk as a confessed preacher was vastly different from prior experiences of Christianity. The expectations of the people and my expectations of myself were so very high. My problem was that I did not have a female role model, who was a preacher who was married with children, in the Baptist denomination. I knew about preachers who were female, in the A.M.E. denomination since I was a child. Baptist was hard.

Reverend Dr. Cheryl Price was the first woman that Pastor Hicks licensed and ordained at Metropolitan. I hoped when God called and ordained Dr. Cheryl that I had made a mistake; that God wanted her and not me. I also helped others who were male to be licensed and ordained.   Dr. Cheryl had the wonderful distinction that she was born and grew up in Metropolitan; and spent her formative years there before going off to college. Her grandmother, Mrs. Lena Price Smith, was well known for her long and distinctive service as the Chairperson of Christian Education.

At the time, Dr. Cheryl was single and away at school. I lived out the whole process of my call as a married woman with children, in an open arena at Church. The unique thing that I can truly say is that Dr. Hicks and most of our Metropolitan family were fully supportive of our family and ministry. I prayed for those who put stumbling blocks in my way, and in the paths of others. Just be the best preacher that I could be was my final resolve. With marriage and three children, accepting the call was a challenging feat. The Holy Spirit was unbelievably amazing.

The worse part about preaching the initial sermon was that there were so many messages stockpiled in my spirit that accumulated through the years. I couldn't choose which one to preach. To find my voice was difficult. That would take a while, and absolute dependence on God the Holy Spirit. The search for authenticity to preach through the voice that God gave me was made more difficult because I kept getting in the way. First of all, I didn't like the sound of my voice. I still don't like it. I thought my voice should sound a certain way when all we have to do is open our mouths, and let the Lord speak for us as God promised Moses in Exodus 4:12; and Jesus told His disciples in Matthew 10:20. Three years in Seminary to help with necessary preparation was a must do for me.   Pastor Hicks required that. In the meantime, God protected me like the Good Shepherd.   It is written:

Psalm 119:114 – "Thou art my hiding place and my shield: I hope in thy Word."

Matthew 10:20 – "For it will not be you speaking, but the Spirit of your Father speaking through you."

To a packed Church, I preached the initial sermon entitled, "The Chronicles of a Would Be Preacher". The Grace of God and the loving-kindness of God's people were overwhelming. The sermon on the other hand... Let's just say I struggled. This time, Deacon Horne made the motion to license me. Several Deacons and a large number of people in the congregation who were not supposed to second the motion, voiced their second, again. That was funny, again.

The only license form available in the market at the time said "he". There was nothing that said "she" or was gender neutral. Afterwards, Dr. Hicks directed me to redesign the preaching license, and to add the Metropolitan logo. That was amazing. I redesigned my own license, and the one that many preachers subsequently received. Change happened in moments that were once "forever" to "suddenly". Three years later, the same would be true for the Certificate of Ordination, which was changed to include women and men. The things that happened to fully bring women into ministry in the Baptist denomination were many. Requesting a robe that was specifically designed to fit a preacher who is female was major. That took a while.

What happened next is a description of outright satanic assault. Believe it or not, the enemy still persisted to prevent me from preaching. Dr. Hicks required that all preachers must go to Seminary who he licensed and ordained. One morning after I was licensed, I had the unmitigated gall to say to God: "Okay, so... I will call the Divinity School. The time is way past the deadline for application to be received for the fall semester, assuming I would be accepted. But, if I get admitted within three days, I will go."

How ridiculous was that? I just knew I could not get an

appointment. So, I sat in my office and called the Howard University School of Divinity. Guess what? As with Dr. Fabro that day when I called his office, Dean Clarence Newsome answered the telephone. Well! That's right. An appointment for the next day was made to see Dean Newsome. OUCH! Things were out of my hands; and I could feel that imaginary steam-roller behind me.

After Dean Newsome's very encouraging conversation, I applied and was admitted to the School of Divinity within three days. Ha! God is so much God that God does not mind if we put the fleece out like Gideon in Judges 6:36-40. Now, faith in Jesus Christ and our obedience to Him makes the fleece most unnecessary, most of the time. We must depend on the God of Jesus Christ, no matter what. Needless to say, I was stunned. I could sense God smiling at me, and the angels, too.

I went to fall orientation for the new students. Everything was happening way too fast. Thinking straight was not working well for me. I was over-the-top with excitement, and yet, at the same time, humbled to the ground at the prospects of being a preacher in Seminary. I sat through the entirety of Orientation, and felt fully prepared to start class. There was one problem. When it came time to pay fees, I realized that my husband and I had not talked about that. I was to pay cash, but at that moment, I had no money. Enrollment would have to wait until everything was placed "decently and in order". There could be no confusion.

On the way back to the Church that was only fifteen minutes away, I got lost. I knew the way back from the Howard Divinity School like the back of hand. My first Masters was earned at Howard. Through the most hellacious taunting of the enemy, I remained lost for over four hours. That day, the demonic forces of darkness were unleashed against me; and they attempted to destroy me. I could literally feel the presence of darkness in the car with me. I was in the midst of full blown spiritual warfare. Out of the corner of my eye, I fought to focus on the large brass cross that held a prominent place in my car, and the need to get to the House of God.

Something terribly evil attempted to come over me to destroy me. I knew it. To say I had a total avalanche of emotions to engulf me would be barely accurate to describe the weight of the event. The comparison could be made to being severely lost in a haunted house that you could not exit in your own backyard. Maddening was that day that experience. In a sense, the experience of being lost became a metaphor for my life prior my confession. How could I be so close and yet so far? But, the confession was made and the initial sermon was preached. God granted me the greatest awakening I had ever known. AND, the hounds of hell were unleashed to destroy me. Don't play. I wanted to tearfully whale.

The enemy attacked like never before. Only God was in control. I was not. I would not doubt. I fought against the spirit of fear, but the spirit of love, power and a sound seemed elusive at that moment. There is a reason "FEAR NOT" is commanded so many times in God's Holy Word. The enemy's attempted assault against the daughters and sons of God is relentless. Constant faith in God and God's Word win, even when the appearance is otherwise. I prayed to God to rescue me and get me to the Church. The attack was deadly. "Please Father! Get me to Your Church."

Suddenly, after more than four hours, God answered my prayers. The way just opened up like nothing ever happened, and I was at Metropolitan in a matter of minutes. The streets which were previously jam packed suddenly became clear. As lost as I was, everything was suddenly bright, familiar and calm, as if nothing happened. God took me to the Church where I attempted to go for hours. Revival was scheduled to start shortly. Clearly, I looked catatonic when I walked in the office from the reaction of some of the staff and church members who saw me. Quite a distinction from my normal personal or professional affect displays, I was later told, I appeared as if I had been in some life-threatening situation or released from aliens. I had.

Dr. Hicks and most of the staff were there, waiting for the Revival, as I would have been. They expected to hear a very different report about school than the one I gave them. Instead, I just kept crying and babbling something about I was lost, which I am sure, made no sense. I called my husband to tell him what happened; and to change the evening plans to bring our children to me. I was going home – my safe place. Like everyone else, I just needed to stop by the Church, first. Those were alien spirits of darkness that I had never encountered before. "FEAR NOT!"

Once more, God created another position for me on staff. The sudden and exponential growth of the Church necessitated that Dr. Hicks appoint me to be Director of Church Ministries. That was a huge assignment. It is true as it is written. Your gifts do make room for you. STAY READY. Use what you have. God processes us to where we need to be. Surrender to the process. I later enrolled in Seminary for spring semester. Our Comrade, Reverend Patrick Young became Director of Youth Ministries.

It is pretty standard and sound advice from most preachers who have attended Seminary that one should "Hold onto your Jesus" through the process. That advice was received; but it was difficult for me to imagine a class convened without Jesus as the subject of instruction and contemplation. I legitimately learned to recognize both the Jesus of Faith and Jesus of History. The love for both presentations of Christ was all encompassing. I honestly admit that I really NEEDED to learn more about the Jesus of

History. It took a while before God the Holy Spirit permitted me to embrace the part of my Theology that was missing. God the Holy Spirit was rarely, if ever, a part of the discussions, however.

Musings with God the Holy Spirit!

- Those who say spiritual warfare is not real have never done or said anything that the enemy views as a threat to the kingdom of darkness.
- Ephesians 6 clearly states that the warfare is real.
- Christians must armor-up with the Word of God as our sure defense, according to Ephesians 6:11.
- The battle is not with humans, according to Ephesian 6:12.
- The demonic forces are strategically aligned.
- Ephesians 6:10-24 teach born-again Christians how to be Victorious, daily, over dark spirits.
- We must remain aligned with God the Holy Spirit with every breath we inhale and exhale.
- Prayer is our sure defense.
- Prayer prepares believers for victory.
- The Word of GOD and prayer win every time.
- Spend no time getting even with anyone about anything.
- Spend time to seek righteousness.
- Do the will of God.
- The spirits of darkness seek to ambush the children of God.
- Stay thankful in prayer for God's protection.
- We are the beneficiaries of Grace through Jesus Christ, our Savior and Lord.
- Grace is God's magnanimous act of love.

Chapter 10
Oh God!
The Preacher's Birth is Scorned!

Deuteronomy 20:1 - "When thou goest out to battle against thine enemies, and seest horses, and chariots, and a people more than thou, be not afraid of them: for the Lord thy God is with thee, which brought thee up out of the land of Egypt."

Mark 6:11 - "And whosoever shall not receive you, nor hear you, when ye depart thence, shake off the dust under your feet for a testimony against them. Verily I say unto you, it shall be **more** tolerable for Sodom and Gomorrah in the Day of Judgment, than for that city."

Acts 1:17 - "And it shall come to pass in the last days, saith God, I will pour out of my Spirit upon all flesh: and your sons and your daughters shall prophesy, and your young men shall see visions, and your old men shall dream dreams."

We read about suffering for followers of Jesus Christ in the Bible and extra Biblical texts or books like the *Book of the Martyr*. More contemporary suffering of Christians is recorded in books and periodicals like *Voice of the Martyrs*. The stories are horrific. So, what I write here in this chapter is hardly worth mentioning. The truth is that while there was opposition to my birth as a preacher, there were countless blessings, which were and are far more important. My obligation to God, my family, and all the people who supported me was to focus on God, and not those who opposed me. The opposition was there as the thorn in my flesh to remind me to glorify God. I didn't always do that great with that assignment. I am yet a work in progress, but to glorify God with all of me is priority, regardless. And, my motto that plays continuously in my spirit is this. "If God ain't in it, I ain't either." That perspective helps to keep me on the trail for God.

The scriptures that are placed at the beginning of this chapter helped me to sharpen my sword in the days that followed my initial sermon. One by one, different people stopped by my office, over the course of several weeks, to share their thoughts and affirm my call. I was humbled and so very grateful. The ones that I appreciated in a very special way were the ones who told me that up to that point in time, they didn't believe that God called women to preach. God changed their minds through what God did through me, and the ministry we performed. There was no way that I could afford to let the negative opinions of people stop me, and my ability to do ministry. The women in ministry who came before me, in all denominations, and the women in the first century church, helped to keep me focused. When I tell you that Mary Magdalene became my best friend, please believe me.

A few male parishioners came by my office, with the Bible in their hands, to say to this poor little lady that they had Bible facts to prove women should not preach. Each time, I simply thanked them for sharing their thoughts, and for their concern about me going to hell. To be honest, neither the men in the Church or outside the Church opposed me and my call to preach the loudest. My greatest opposition came from some of the other women.

There was this one lady who was a long-time member of the

congregation. I can only surmise why she was marginalized until after God directed me to bring her closer into the fold of ministry. Though there was some uneasiness on my part about her, she pretended she was my friend. To permit her friendship was my decision. One Sunday, after I was licensed, the woman literally became someone else. She walked up to where I was teaching and slapped me. Where and why she mounted that much vengeance toward me, I will never know. I taught the new members class of 50 plus people, after the 11:00 a.m. service. She stunned and blindsided me, as my face literally rattled from the irrational, unprovoked, action.

Very quickly, I took a smooth, deep breath and kept teaching without interruption. In that room that day were people from all walks of life who had just united with the Church of Jesus Christ. Many were new converts who needed to see Christianity in action. Therefore, God the Holy Spirit did not permit me to skip a beat, as everyone looked on with utter bewilderment. The devil literally came over that woman. Thank God there were other prayer partners present, and some members of our Victorious Christian Living Bible Class. They stood near me, in silence and strength, from which I drew strength. I fed off of their Godly energy.

The next day, my Comrades laughed about the incident some more; and poked more fun at me. That was still unbelievable, but we cracked up laughing. The Comrades always laugh a lot at life. So, I coined this phrase to describe what they mean to me. The phrase says: "When everyone else says I'll see you later, the Comrade say we'll see you through." They are all happily married, Godly, hard-working preachers who are male. God brought them to Metropolitan to serve, and gifted all of us to be yokefellows to this day. Their wives and my husband are Comrades too. We made each other's ministry easier to accomplish. As a preacher who is female, I have them to thank because they are great preachers who embraced my call at a time when it was most unpopular to do so. The congregation celebrated our unity

Who wants to talk about turn the other cheek? God the Holy Spirit has helped me turn the other cheek so much, I should have permanent whiplash. Randomly, I still wonder did God let me bring that woman that close just so she could be present to slap me. (Smile!) ONLY because of the power of God in action, I never treated that church member any differently afterwards. That incident turned out to be one of the most valuable lessons of them all about Church people from a preacher's point of view. More lessons would follow in rapid succession. Those lessons were on some heavenly manifest of things to do.

A part of me wanted to be the same person that I was before I confessed the call; preached the initial sermon; and was licensed. I wanted to pretend that nothing changed, but the truth was that absolutely everything changed. Learning to live with that would take God the Holy Spirit to teach me. People attempt to put preachers in a place; and expect you to stay there in that place; and be that, whatever that is that they decide you should be. I was never the person who fit another person's mold. However, there was this tendency on my part to want to convince people that God was just "adding" another role, but I knew better. Like the Apostle Paul said, "I die dally". Each of us must. However, most people do not; and some resented the fact that I did, of necessity. I was on Kingdom assignment, acting normal, but dying daily. That Godly process empowers us.

As a result of the new life to which God took me, everything changed. The truth of 2 Corinthians 5:17 had a new application for me as a preacher. On the other hand, it was as if there was a bull's eye on my back that suddenly got even wider than it was when I was a working Christian. Clearly, we move up on the enemy's hit list once the line is crossed to become a preacher. Hit list or not, I had reached vertigo, the point of no return. Neither time nor space permit me to tell about all the grace and power that Almighty God granted to me to handle the "stuff" that a few spirits of darkness hurled at me. Does "stuff" really matter?

Remember! As a preacher, I was determined that my roles as wife and mother would not be compromised. In my head and heart, I worked to become the Proverbs 31 woman, even before becoming a preacher; and even more afterwards. For me, there is nothing worse than the person who is always in Church and the spouse, children and home are a mess. Such a scenario was unacceptable to me. Everyone knew that God, husband and family were and yet are my priority. I never compromised on that,

Competing against other people is useless and never my style. Rather, from my youth, God showed me that my role is to be an encourager who employs a standard of Godly excellence in all things. I slept for three hours each night; woke, prayed and studied; showered and dressed; and arrived at the church by 6:30 a.m. That way, I could get in the express lanes from D.C. to Fairfax by 2:30 p.m. I would pull into the driveway, either just before or just after our children arrived home from school. To this routine, Divinity School was added. For three years, I drove 120 miles a minimum of three days a week. Before dawn, I drove to work; drove home; got our sons and daughter fed; got them to a sitter or a sitter to them; and drove back to Washington to attend classes for two or three hours; drove to the sitters to pick up our children; and then drove home. Immediately, when a preacher tells me something is too difficult, I tune all the way out, in a hurry.

To say I was ecstatic to be in the Howard University School of

Divinity would be a major understatement. Like the Prophetess Anna in Luke 2:26-28, if I were younger and single without children, I simply would have moved into the living quarters and camped out in the sacred halls, day and night. That way I could absorb all of the knowledge, wisdom and revelation from the professors, and from the other students. Without a doubt, the Seminary years were some of the most challenging years of my life; but they were also some of the best. God grew me so rapidly and widely that the experience is indescribable. Again, the challenges were many, but minor when we consider what Jesus did, the early Church founders. However, our challenges are our challenges, and should not be minimized in the face of some grander.

My appreciation for Mary Magdalene is more than obvious. Perhaps, accepting my call would have been easier if I had known more about her, earlier, like in young adulthood. Much more was written in the first 20 years after I received my degree. Her love for Jesus as Sovereign Lord was unsurpassed. Women and men should study her life as the woman who the early Theologian and historian St. Augustine and the Catholic Church designated as the "Apostle to the Apostles", based on John 20:17-18, and Mark 16:1-10. I totally got what God did through the Apostle Mary Magdalene, who left no room for whining or wimping. Women were and have always been front-line servants of Jesus Christ and Christ's Church. Women who serve God as preachers are born-again, spiritual, beautiful, wise, strong, and intelligent; and, at the same time, they are married or single; with children or without children. One size does not fit all, females or males.

A very challenging week during this period was the week that put everything in perspective for me. All of the preachers and some of the staff went to the West Coast for a site visit with Dr.

Robert Schuller at the Crystal Cathedral. One day, while they were gone, I received a call from a man who didn't identify himself. He said that he and some others were watching me, and that they knew all the male staff members were gone. The man said that he and his friends were coming to kill me because a woman shouldn't be a preacher anyway. Deaconess Queen Boyd took the call and connected him to me.

The conversation was most disarming, but I listened to his complaint; and told him that I would share the details of the call with Pastor Hicks when he returned. I thanked the man for calling, and ended the conversation. I learned more profoundly that fear is never an option for believers, especially preachers. Fear diminishes faith and draws the enemy's fire. Nothing happened.

Early one morning in that same week, the director from a local Mortuary called to tell us that one of our former member's service was to be held at 10:00 a.m., that day They wanted someone from the Church to do the eulogy. I didn't know the person, so we went into full press to find out something about her. There was no information whatsoever available about this elderly lady. She was never on any sick list or in any database. No one knew her, including life-long Church members who tithed time and service in the office. With absolutely no information on this poor soul, I rushed over to participate in the service at the funeral home on Capitol Hill. Traffic was horrendous.

When I finally arrived, only fifteen minutes late, the service was over. Blown away by that fact, I felt totally ineffective and woefully defeated. I am obsessive about punctuality. That day I was late. I offered my sincerest condolences and apology to the lone nephew who was the only person there, beside the funeral home staff. The nephew did not receive my condolences; and seemed quite indignant about my tardiness. As cold as ice, the man treated me like dirt, which was apparently how he treated all women. A woman can always tell those guys.

I prayed for the deceased who was being cremated. There was nothing I could do or offer that the nephew accepted. I was late to a funeral for a person we did not know that we just found out was deceased less than two hours earlier. She may have been a member at one time, many years prior, but no one knew her. All of that was the Church's fault. The sad thing for me was that knowledge of her relationship with Jesus Christ was unknown. What was her Christian experience? My mind raced. Where had she been to worship and serve all of those years? I felt defeated and alone. Grief can cause people to act unnecessarily strange. That is how her nephew's behavior was reconciled in my mind.

I had to get back to preach the noonday worship service and handle all of the needs that came up while I was gone. Normally, there would be four preachers and staff in the office. We were down to two highly efficient administrative staff members - Kym Harden and Carmeta Hodge; the custodial staff; volunteers; and me. Traffic was jammed to a standstill because a child was run over and killed, I learned from someone on the street. That fact devastated me. I wanted to stop my car, get out, and do something. But, there was nothing that could be done

Neither the police officers nor time permitted my assistance. I felt like I was that priest who passed by on the other side in the parable of the Samaritan that Luke 10: 25-37 records. I was more concerned about what I had to do than what needed to be done. It was already too late for the child. Imagine the pain I felt for the child and the family, as a mother, and as a Christian. As I passed by, I could see that the body was already covered up and the police wouldn't let me explain to them that I was a preacher and wanted to offer prayer and comfort. He didn't believe me. He did not care. He did not even like me for saying that I was a preacher. He all but growled at me. Wow! Was I being super-sensitive? One learns to discern, quickly who is for you and who is against you. Don't be distracted was God the Holy Spirit's message to me.

Later that same day, after preaching the noonday service and teaching Bible study, my beloved and highly effective Administrative Assistant, Carmeta Hodge, summoned me to the main office, as she always did to handle some unexpected, serious matter. Her call always had the same two words. "Come, quickly!" As usual, I sprinted to the other side in very high heeled shoes. An elderly man was in the main office that lived in the neighborhood, I would learn, though I had never seen him before. He seemed hardened from his years of life; and burdened down by some current situation. He just stood there totally bewildered. Very warmly and professionally, I simply introduced myself to the gentleman using only my first and last name; and asked him how I could assist him.

The man said, "I came over here looking for the preacher. She said she was gon' call the preacher. "

"Yes sir', I said. "Our Administrative Assistant called me to help you. I am one of the preachers."

He was kindly surprised with a curious look on his face that seemed to wonder how was that possible. I was led to take him to the sanctuary, as I often did with walk-ins, so the very environment would minister to them. We sat down on the first pew and he began to talk from a very painful place. Without being crass or rude or macho or anything, but totally humble, he stopped in mid-conversation and said, "I didn't know that the preacher was gon' be a woman."

I smiled and asked him if I, a woman, was alright? He humbly and politely said yes, that in fact it helped him. He talked on for a while. I carefully listened. Then, with this look of relief on his face, he said, "If God could make a woman a preacher, then he can probably help me." I smiled and simply said, "I'm very sure God can help you." The man's humility and innocence mingled with his desire to know Jesus grabbed me in my imaginary clergy collar. A major production, orchestrated in heaven, occurred. All of it was orchestrated for the man's one simple question, "Is Jesus real?" Somehow, the fact that I was a preacher who was female gave him the answer that was desired and needed. God sent this wonderful stranger to me.

For me, the kindly gentleman represented all the people to whom I was sent that I had not met yet. There were so many like him who came through our doors each week; and so many like him at Central Union Missions where we ministered down the street and elsewhere. For the next hour, I sat with him and shared with him the story of Jesus in a way that he could understand. We prayed together. I offered him the Salvation of Jesus Christ. He accepted. I concluded with the story of the thief on the cross, and that I believed if Jesus came that night, in whatever way, that he would go to heaven. He was overjoyed. That was a blessed end to a terrible day. God saw all of it. I drove home, later than usual.

That day, I learned in a brand new way, what God had slowly revealed over the course of years on my pilgrimage to become a preacher. Expect the unexpected. Pay attention to what seems to be the unscripted things. The scripted stuff is rather obvious. The unscripted things, from our perspective, are on God's manifest of things that we will encounter, and what God's result will be. When we pay attention, we see the hand of God. All will work out according to God's plan. However, it's easier if we get it right the first time to avoid unnecessary delays in our flight.

As a minister, I started to do hospital and shut-in visits with my Comrade, Reverend William Harris, who was the Assistant to the Senior Minister. On this particular day, a very faithful elderly member of long standing was admitted to the Washington Hospital Center in serious condition. Clergy could visit patients anytime – all clergy except me it seemed. That was because the security guard at the desk refused to permit me to go visit our member, before visiting hours, though I used the title Minister to sign in. I very politely and professionally told him that I was clergy.

Straight out, the guard said that he did not believe a woman could be a preacher. He got really angry with me for saying I was a preacher. His behavior was crazy. Even as Reverend Harris vouched for me, the guard threatened me with arrest if I went upstairs; but Reverend Harris was treated nicely. At least I knew how clergy should be treated as a member of the healing team.   I said, "Okay. Arrest me. But, I'm going to see the saint, first. Call for backup. You will know where to find me".

When we arrived in the room, we could tell immediately that the patient was indeed very ill. But, as soon as she saw us, the whole countenance of this 95 year old saint changed before our eyes. Joy swept over the room, and all of us. That's what the enemy attempted to prevent - transformational joy for a child of God. I jokingly told her about what just happened; why I wasn't going to let the guard stop me from seeing her; and that I might go to jail because of her. The instance was like telling your Mother about some bully who picked on you at school and you beat him up. I chose to tell her that because I knew her well, and knew that detail would energize her. She came to my defense.

The wonderful senior saint really got a kick out of that story. She encouraged us in ministry in a remarkable way, like she was

137

not sick at all. She said we had to keep up the fight for the Lord. Surely, she had. We joked and laughed about my episode until we cried. We prayed for her with the fullness of joy. You have to know the family of God to know what can and cannot be said. I knew she would appreciate hearing about exploits because she was a woman who fought to overcome obstacles in government and civil rights in her day. She was always so supportive of us. She was a true preacher's friend. There was nothing that I could learn from a book about congregational care that we didn't live all day, every day, 24 hours a day, seven (7) days a week at Metropolitan.

The angels kept us guarded because it took about 30 minutes before we knew someone official was coming down the hall. That was funny. We stayed as long as we should, uninterrupted. In this profession, one learns even more than normal how to see and hear everything. I could hear the angry footsteps of three out of shape security people. "Ooops! Here they come to get me", I said. We laughed some more; prayed again, quickly; gave her a kiss; and dashed out the door before they could get to her room. I will always remember that we left each other laughing that day. Reverend Harris and I laughed all the way back to the Church. A few days later, she passed. Her home-going service was amazing, as she deserved. Dr. Hicks is an expert eulogist.

My husband, children and I attended the Pastor and First Lady's Anniversary at the Shoreham Hotel. We exchanged greetings and brief conversations with members of the congregation, as we passed through the large crowd of people in the lobby, and made our way into the ballroom. I overheard a long-time male member of the congregation say with great disdain: "Look at her. She says God called her to be a preacher. Sho' don't look like no preacher to me." I hoped my husband and children did not here what he said. If they did, they didn't understand. I never turned around, though I knew the voice. Every time I saw him in Church, I spoke to him, as he turned his back on me. No one ever corrected him. The people who listened to him were his people, and to that group of people I was an outsider in Metropolitan, and forever would be, according to them.

Several weeks later, a call came into the Church, and it was transferred to me. It was the police. That same man was found dead in his apartment. Apparently, he had been there for several days, in the sweltering heat. His body had badly decomposed and they needed someone to identify him. I did. I felt sad that his life ended like that. I participated in his service, as a part of my job; and went to the service of committal at the gravesite. I expressed condolences to "his people" who surprisingly began to warm up. God was making me a preacher through some very unwelcomed lessons that I had to learn, quickly.

When Dr. Hicks licensed and later ordained the first woman, Reverend Cheryl Price, he was put out of one of the Ministers' Conferences. A few years passed while God moved me forward, and I got my act together for licensing. Just when the ministers thought it was safe to invite him back into the Conference, Dr. Hicks licensed me. When the letter came to invite him back, Dr. Hicks said he would return if he could bring Minister Nawanna Lewis Miller with him. That ended that. No deal!!

One day, Dr. Hicks instructed the Comrades and me that we were to go to a luncheon with him for at one of the Baptist Ministers' Conferences. "Who has time for that", I thought to myself. Needless to say, I objected. I knew some of the ministers with whom I had a good working relationship in the community before I was licensed. (I sneak in a laugh right here. No disrespect intended!) After I was licensed, they treated me differently, like I was a leper. Truth is I just did not feel like being the object of their disdain that day. Nevertheless, as we entered the lobby to the fellowship hall of the Church where the luncheon was held, I lingered back. Knowing me well as they did, my Comrades knew I was up to something. I assured them everything was fine, and that I definitely would be inside in a minute. They walked to their table and sat down.

Of course many of the ministers, all male, made their way over to speak to Dr. Hicks, and to exchange pleasantries with the other Comrades. I gagged on the flamboyant hypocrisy from the good ole boys network, just before I entered the room. What happened next was akin to mass cardiac arrest. Some of the preachers stopped in mid-sentence, and just looked, but they lived to talk about me being there. Others, got quiet very quickly; and still others fumed with disgust after they were revived. You could hear the proverbial church mouse relieve itself on cotton. That whole situation was hilarious to me, one of my best moments in strength training for the preachers' assignment. The reality was that change had come to the Baptist denomination, and that was only the beginning. Many waited to see the outcome of my call.

While maintaining proper decorum most of the time, the Comrades just never knew what I would do, as long as I perceived it to be in Godly order. I spoke very graciously and professionally to the preachers, as I entered. Some of them made it clear that I was not welcomed at the luncheon. Others did not know how to respond. These were probably fence straddlers. Clearly, all of them weighed the change already in progress. Some were not opposed to preachers who are female. They weighed their next step. I wanted those ministers to understand that I walk alone with God, under the Biblical authority of my husband, with our children, and the friends God raises up for me. They saw first-hand that their male opposition in no way intimidated me; or determined under their breath God's will for my life. Undoubtedly, the message, though silent, was heard and broadcasted loudly and clearly. The fake ones really were and are a bit much.

If I could have stood up and given them a soliloquy, it would have included the fact that a woman is here to do God's ministry, and more women are on their way. I would have told them to exclude women from your little group, if you want, but you cannot exclude us from the King, the Kingdom, or the King's work. I would have told them that I understand that as a woman, I am a threat only to insecure men's misappropriation of perceived power. I would have told them that I understand why they attempted to silence women from preaching for so long. I would have told them about their futile intent to hold onto some illegitimate power that Peter and the other Apostles also sought to maintain and to hinder women. I would have told them that the spiritual daughters of the Apostle Mary Magdalene keep coming, with the immeasurable Gifts of God the Holy Spirit, to use for greater works, including Proclamation of the Gospel. I would have told them that the Bible is clear that God did and does call women. I would have told them the preachers who are women that God calls and sends are not the silly women of 2 Timothy 3:6. I would have told them that the preachers who are women are phenomenal women who love, obey, and serve God. I would have told them that because God calls women and uses women that the balance and order of the universe is set in motion. I would have told them that the preachers who are women have the same fortitude of the women at the cross who heard the Seven Last Sayings of Christ from the Cross for themselves. But, God was speaking. And, because God spoke, their all male bastions of self-aggrandizement were drying up. Real men support women, and vice versa.

For me, that day was an Apostle Peter and Apostle Mary Magdalene kind of moment. The blessing of Grace was that I saw Jesus in the most incredibly amazing ways for myself through my struggle to accept the call. In the spirit, non-verbally, I said to them, "You just do not want to believe that women can hear from God, and know something that Jesus told a woman and not you." I would have told them that I get it. As soon as a preacher who is a woman enters the room, men have to change the conversation like you did today, which most likely was not about God in the first place. The Spirit of Discernment is real. I KNOW YOUR MOTIVES. I am WOMAN who is wife, mother, preacher.

At the foot of the cross is common ground to which each of us must walk, as proclaimers of Divine Truth – preachers, every time that Truth is proclaimed. From there, we walk to the empty tomb on Resurrection morning. From the tomb, we walk where God the Holy Spirit sends us to proclaim that Jesus is alive. Jesus has already gone ahead of us. These are the thoughts that came to my spirit, soul, and body that day. Those are always my distant thoughts that are only reluctantly uncovered when I see someone pathetically attempt to invalidate a preacher who is female. Who is worthy to judge whether someone thinks women should or can preach? Really? To tell the truth, that was the day that I let "them", all of "them" go. What their opinion of my call might be did not matter. I had fun doing that unanticipated act of speaking the truth in love with my presence. Thank God.

Lest you think differently, the scorning of a few in no way ever overshadowed the support of the many. I had to deal with rejection for the first time in my life, but I had a husband and children who loved me and breathed life into me. I had the sons and daughters, of all ages and stages who were there for me. One of my staunchest supporters was Reverend Dr. H. Beecher Hicks, Sr. of Columbus, Ohio who was the father of our Pastor. He is the original Daddy Hicks who is now a citizen of heaven. Daddy Hicks never left the city without depositing an encouraging word. One day, as a loving father, he very casually shared a statement with me that was life altering.

Daddy Hicks said, "Baby! Never let them see you as a woman preacher. Always make sure that they see you as a preacher who happens to be a lady." That statement sank deeply into the very fabric of my soul as an anchor from God. It is one of the golden truths that I treasure and live each day. Since Metropolitan was engaged in major ministry, locally, nationally, and internationally, I could not diminish in any way God's great gift to me to serve there; accept my call there; and grow there.

Like Daddy Hicks, Deacon Horne always made his Monday morning visits to see how Pastor Hicks and the ministry were doing. He also checked on how each of us who were staff was doing. The lessons that he taught us through casual conversations and the encouragement that he gave the staff are forever treasurers in my head, and heart, as well. Deacon Horne and the Comrades always laughed about everything, no matter how bad things were. He was one of the sure defenders of the faith who looked out for all of us who were clergy. One Sunday, that defense was taken to a whole new level. I shouldn't tell it, but what happened should not have happened.

Immediately following the second service one Sunday, the staff was in the crowded office serving parishioners. While still in my robe, one of the Associate Ministers came up to me to question why he was not getting time to serve in the pulpit. The clergy person made a decision that I was the one preventing him from serving during the Sunday morning worship. I explained to him that the pulpit assignments were the responsibility of the Assistant to the Pastor, Reverend Harris, not me. He did not accept that answer from me. Instead, when I told him that, he took a swing at me, and slapped me so hard, I was momentarily off balance. Do you want truth, the real truth? I was ready to fight. Enough was enough.

As a reflex action, I prepared to take him out, before I knew what was happening. Out of nowhere, Deacon Horne grabbed me as I swung; jumped in front of me; and pushed me down in a chair. I kept bucking to get up, saying "but he slapped me". The good Deacon, who saw the entire encounter transpire, kept pushing me back down in the chair; and dared me to move, again. With Deacon Horne's very able assistance, God did not permit me to fall prey to the enemy; and cause volatile scene to escalate.

The man was so angry at me for something that was not my fault that he forgot his kids in the nursery and had to come back through the office doors to get them. The other sides were locked. By then, I was spiritually where I needed to be, but still fighting my flesh. God's angel was still standing in front of me when the preacher breezed past us. I let it go and settled in my spirit that the test was passed. I waited for our Monday morning conversation which was always more than amusing with Deacon Horne. From that point onward, he often laughed at me, that I was the preacher who vowed to be a lady, but ready to fight like a man. That was true. I was about to lose it.

We received several death threats, for one reason or the other, mostly from members who had emotional issues of one kind or another. One day, after one of those threats, I suddenly realized how every Sunday preachers on the pulpit are literally sitting ducks for anyone who was is having a bad day to pluck off. I turned all of that over to God, as we all did.

Our Church was located in the heart of what was once a middle class section of Washington, but had become one of the nation's worse corridors for drugs and prostitution. Our Street Ministries was birthed as a result of service to the people who entered our Church doors every single day to get help. We helped them. The people were the "Anawim", the least, the lost, the last, and the left out. We represented Christ. Most all of them called me Mama. Warm thoughts flood my mind about my street people and some of their antics. The Anawim were known to be my people, and they protected me on the streets in that area. We loved each other. While everyone did not get saved, many did. We introduced Christ; and everyone who came down our path received attention and love. In addition to Central Union Mission, we worked with the phenomenal Mitch Snyder to provide services to homeless people. Direct service to people in need was a way of daily life for our ministry.

The men of Metropolitan like Mr. Jimmy Morgan, Deacon Clarence Branson and others became our security guards during the week, on the side of the complex where I was. They thought that I took way too many risks. I will always remember what Mr. Morgan said to me one day after I finished ministering to a woman who was a prostitute. That day she washed up in the ladies restroom. I had to let her know that was not okay. (She finally got saved, by the way.) But, that day, Mr. Morgan said, "Baby, you can't help all these people. It's too dangerous. But, I know you won't quit. So, I tell you what. Old Jimmy gone watch, while you pray. That's all I can do."

Mr. Morgan was right. That was how we ministered from then onward. Those words became a cornerstone of ministry for me to this day. For me that day, it was a new take on the instructions in Matthew 26:41. God had already begun the birth of Street Ministries in me, and we didn't know it. Some commented that Metropolitan didn't have all those homeless people coming through until I started tending to them. Ha! That is true. Later, God sent to us Reverend Robert Linden to lead our Street Ministries that became one of the models in the country. Deacon Husie Cross continued to manage the food distribution ministry in a more excellent way. That did not hinder our daily walk-ins.

One Sunday, as soon as the benediction was pronounced, this man from the Middle East made his way toward the pulpit shouting something that had to be obscenities toward me, as detected from the tone in his voice. Four other male preachers and I stood at the altar to greet the congregation after service, but the man goes after me in a verbal rage. I guess he didn't think I should be up there either. Speaking in tongues helped me that day. I walked out from the other clergy and congregants, and apparently spoke in his language, in Spiritual Tongues, though I did not know what that language was. How God the Holy Spirit spoke and completely diffused the danger that was present, still arrests my thoughts to this day. The man calmed all the way down, and Security took him away.

That event was similar to the day when we pulled up to the Church, after a service of committal. This homeless man with mental issues was in Metropolitan's flower bed pulling up flowers. He kept filling up a water bottle and dumping the water on the flowers he pulled up and his head. The Comrades attempted to reason with him to stop his antics without success. He literally snarled at me when he used the "N" word. Normal, loving, kind, preacherly responses left me. Into the Spiritual Gift of Tongues I went. God did not permit me to think. I looked directly at a demon possessed man and I knew it. No intellectual strategy would work. God the Holy Spirit totally handled that situation. I seriously didn't know what happened until later that day when Reverend Harris came to my office to explain, after we literally served the bereaved family the repast in the fellowship hall. That was one of those weird, unexplainable moments when you did not pray for God to do anything. Rather, God just takes over to work through you. That can be really freaky to say the least, until you learn to stay out of God's way.

I had a similar experience when I first became the Director of Youth Ministries. I planned a lock-in for the teens which some in leadership opposed, but Dr. Hicks permitted. Many ministers over the years have told me that Metropolitan was at the forefront for relevant, cutting edge ministry. Many traditions had to gently but persuasively give way for God's new thing to take place. Much to my surprise and dismay, for weeks, I dreamed that I was a Ninja. That's right, a Ninja. As crazy as that sounds, I was fighting like a real Ninja warrior or something in all of these dreams, and winning. I could not interpret the dream, as I usually did.

That night of the lock-in, all the female adults who agreed to help me chaperone the teenage girls cancelled out. But, I couldn't disappoint the youth and decided to go forward with the ministry event. The male chaperones were there including the Sunday School Superintendent, Freddie Vaughn; Marion Phillips; and my good brother and Comrade, Reverend Casey Kimbrough. Around 3:00 a.m., all of a sudden, everyone started to get extremely sleepy. We separated the boys from the girls and put cots across the doorways so no one could open the doors or move without bumping into the cot that contained an adult chaperone. God said, "Put your purse under your back." I did as I was told.

In a matter of minutes, it was like someone sprinkled some

sleep dust on us or something. Everyone was sound asleep. All of a sudden, in less than five minutes, I felt a hand go under my back. Though in a zipped-up sleeping bag, asleep, God brought me straight out of that sleeping bag like a bullet, without unzipping it. I grabbed the person who attempted to rob me, and penned her to the wall. Her hands were penned over her head like I was a real police person, instead of a suburban housewife. Smile!

The woman was one of the local ladies of the evening, a prostitute, who the custodian brought in and we did not know it. As I called out to the brethren to help me, they woke up looking completely dazed and confused. They attempted to figure out what in the world I was up to now., as Reverend Kimbrough said. God let me actually become the Ninja who was in my dream. That too changed me forever. God warned me in the dreams. God gave me supernatural ability to move out of the sleeping bag, without unzipping it; and pen the woman to the wall. God gave me strength and power to do what I otherwise could not do. Oh, how I knew forever that God watches over us.

Shocking was the day that the telephone rang, and as usual, the familiar words, "Come quickly" were uttered from the lip of Carmeta. When I arrived at the main office in the Administration Building, Kym Harden, our Church Secretary, was talking to the woman who desperately needed help. The petite woman was dressed only in a slip, with no shoes on her feet in the middle of a very cold winter day, but sunny. The office staff had summoned Ricky and Chase to go to another building to find clothes, shoes and a coat from the clothing supply for the woman. I took her to my office, out of public view while other staff members prayed and handled all of my requests regarding her. WE WERE THE GREATEST MINISTRY TEAM EVER.

When the woman was warmed and felt safe, she began to share

her story. According to her, a U.S. Congressman held her against her will at a penthouse apartment in Arlington, Virginia. She fled and ran all the way to the Church, during the course of late night and the early morning hours, hiding from anyone who might threaten her to be recaptured. She was a sex slave. I asked her for the number of her parents or family so that I could call them let them know that she was alive.

The young woman gave me the number to her home in Florida. When the woman answered the telephone, somewhat pensively, I explained who I was and why I was calling. The person broke down into painful sobs. Apparently, a few days before I called, the Mother and Father of this young woman came to D.C. to look for their daughter. They were in the area close to the Church. Fully dressed, the young woman went with me into the Noon Day Worship Service to wait for the reunion with her parents, after several years. God is faithful. She mostly slept during that time, but it was most definitely a God ordained moment when her parents were reunited with their child. There is no way to measure the magnitude of God's Divine Power and Wisdom.

It was late in the afternoon one day when the telephone rang. It was Dr. Hicks. He wanted to let me know that he sent Minister Donell Peterman to me to get him involved formerly in the Metropolitan Ministries. I finished up the call with my back to the door, as I almost simultaneously yelled come in to the knocker. I turned around in the high backed chair to greet the man. As I did so, this young adult male seemed taken off guard. He later told the story on several occasions about the first time he met me, a woman, who was a preacher, in high heeled shoes.

Whenever a member came to us and said she or he wanted to work, even more a preacher, we thankfully put that member to work. I talked to Minister Peterman in depth about how he could work in the ministry, in a matter of minutes. We had to be efficient time managers, and we had the Heavenly Host to help us discern what was what and who was who to protect the flock and the spirit of unity that flowed between the staff. All of a sudden an urgent knock on the door startled me as Carmita entered.

"COME QUICK. SHE IS CUTTING HERSELF WITH A BLADE AND BLEEDING ALL OVER EVERY WHERE. WE CALLED THE POLICE... " she said. I was already in full stride when I told Minister Peterman to come on, and he ran with us to the other side. DeAnna Daniels, our Social Services Director, was there.

When we got there, things were as described. The woman was outside under the carillon wielding a switch bade, and daring the police to approach her. I walked up to her under the power of God the Holy Spirit. Speaking in Tongues, I commanded that spirit to lose her Drop the blade. Come out of her. And let her go. It did. D.C. Police took over and the ambulance took the woman who became calm and innocent to the hospital.

Reverend Peterman tells the story from his point of view, which is quite hysterical, since all ended well. He says that he is from Dania, Florida and had never seen a woman preacher. He says when he watched from the bushes, God made a convert out of him to believe that God calls women to but preach. We walked back into the office with Reverend Peterman still in shock. I said to him what Pastor Hicks said to me and Reverend Kimbrough and me when we handled a similar case. "Welcome to urban ministries", I said, as I hurried to get in the express lanes before rush hour and finish my routine. By the way, that was the day that I was late for one of my favorite professors' class about which I tell you next. HA

From all of those moments in ministry and countless others, some better and many worse, God birthed and grew a spiritual warrior, but I didn't know that. I was pregnant with my real self. Ministry at its best is on the job training, daily. No two scenarios are the same. There are as many scenarios as there are people who must be served. Only God the Holy Spirit can prepare us to do what God called us to do. Scorning is a part of the process. Spiritual bullies are a part of the process. Uncertainty about what God is doing is a frequent a part of the process. Our call is to obedience and faithfulness. Just be faithful to the process of God. God births what God the Holy Spirit seeded before the foundation of the world. Spiritual warrior notwithstanding, fatigue in labor can get the best of us to the point where we want to quit mid-process. Quitting is not God's will. IF God brought us to the process, God will grant the victory through the process. God delivers us. God restores us. God advances us.

There was this one point when I was so close to finishing Seminary, but overwhelming obstacles got in the way. The work at Church, the needs of God's people, the demands of Seminary, the commute, everything, except my husband and children, had all become too much. I stopped typing the research paper that day and went outside to sit under the huge oak tree in our front yard. The day was an incredibly beautiful fall day. All of a sudden, our three children pulled up on bikes, as if someone summoned them. God did. One by one, they began to ask me what was wrong. I began to explain how difficult everything had become, including the long commute in traffic four times a day.

"Mommy does not think that I can continue. I think I will quit Seminary", I said. I told them how I was real clear that their Dad and each of them were my priority ministry; and that ministry at the Church was a priority too. "So", I said, "I guess I will have to quit school."

"Quit?" said George. "Quit?" said John. "Quit?" said Mikah.

"What do you mean quit", they said in unison. (Exactly! What did I mean?) Then, our eleven and twelve year old sons and eight year old daughter proceeded to give me the absolute best lecture of my life. Still straddling their bikes under the oak tree, they began a barrage of statements and questions that seemed to be the summation of a whole lot of things they learned when I did not think they listened about being responsible and finishing well. That was a real cosmic moment, as if the whole encounter was divinely orchestrated. It was. They took turns. When one spoke the other two would agree. "How do you quit?" "We don't quit?" "Don't you work for God?" "How do you tell God you quit?" "God probably won't like that one bit!" "What will God say about you quitting?" "That doesn't sound like an idea God would approve."

The arguments against me quitting were unbelievably sound, with dialogue to support their points. They spoke with the voice of wisdom way beyond their years. I could see the whole thought of me quitting overwhelmed them. They volunteered to help me finish. They already had. The crisis was over. Persevere against all odds and opposition, we taught them. God used our children to work the works. That was an incredible God-moment.

We can never look at the scorners. They are doing what scorners do. Scorn! Rise above it. I will always be grateful to the supporters, especially my husband, children, and Comrades. The Comrades always treated me as equal. I often joke and say that the only thing that made me unequal to them was basketball. They never let me play basketball. I never asked. In everything else, I was equal.

My husband, our children, my Comrades including Dr. Hicks and Reverend H. Wesley Wiley, our Victorious Christian Living Bible Class, and countless special saints at Metropolitan were my

Doulas. No doubt, God chose them for the birth of the preacher. Generally, Doulas facilitate the birth of a child. God taught me that spiritual Doulas facilitate the birth of ministry, visions, dreams, and ideas. Doulas know what to say and what to do; and when to say and do what needs to be done. There was never a moment when my Doulas failed to do or say the right thing, not because I liked it. They were God-chosen and directed people.

Spend no time thinking about those who don't support your call, vision or dream. To engage in such mindless behavior is a power drain over which we must take authority. Visualize what God says through prayer, and in the Holy Word; through revelations and the Word of knowledge through others; and go for God's plan. God has already stationed your Doulas in the place where God will birth that which is assigned to you. Scorners make you strong so God, the Doulas and you can push for delivery.

That day in the front yard with our children we took the word "quit" right out of my vocabulary, forever. We never liked it in the first place. God even uses our children to get God's Will done. God delivered me from myself through the babies the enemy tried to cancel. Literally, God birthed and saved the children who rescued me many times; and most of the time from myself. Ministry was a lifestyle for them. Yet, I will never know the full scope of the other sacrifices my husband and children made to support me in ministry. I do know that my husband George bore the brunt of many crude and unfair jokes about him being married to a preacher. On the other hand, many people greatly admired his support and courage. So does this preacher. Likewise, our sons and daughter were encountered disparaging dialogue and ungodly behavior. They too were surrounded with scorners who were disarmed through the love of my family and supporters.

Chapter 11
Oh God!
The Stretch Marks Creep!

Galatians 6:17-18 – "From henceforth let no man trouble me: for I bear in my body the marks of the Lord Jesus. Brethren, the grace of our Lord Jesus Christ be with your spirit. Amen.

The thing about stretch marks is that you never physically feel the process of them creeping up on your body. They just show up unannounced. Once they take up squatters' rights, for the most part, once there, the assortment of skin discolorations never fully fade away, even if they are only there in your memory. We see them in a rather annoying way. There is always a hint of their presence that remains. They really serve no useful purpose, on the surface, but we should respect them as a reminder of the Miracle of birth that only the Grace of God can perform. They remind us that they are the result of housing a baby who is to be born, or was birthed from a space that is too small for what constantly grows. Stretch marks represent the incredible.

Likewise, in the spirit, what God gives life through us is bigger than we are. God stretches us way beyond our defined limits to accommodate that life, that baby, that ministry, that idea, that vision, that goal or that dream. God delimits us to stretch us beyond our normal capacity to see, do, say, believe, think, plan, and obtain through faith in the God of Jesus Christ. If all you have faith in is you, and what you can do, you have a milk dud as your partner and not a true visionary. We work with God the Holy Spirit from within to procreate with the Creator of all things, visible and invisible, especially the call to preach.

What I learned through the years, with greatly previsioned and precise detail, is that God already connected that labyrinth of people, places and things that will bless God's daughters and sons, for God's glory and our good. When we make that next connection, a light comes on in an important room in our lives to illumine the way to the next point of contact. We must stay tuned in to the will of God; God's messages; and the Light of God the Holy Spirit. We receive more enlightenment from the constant unfolding of Biblical knowledge and God's new revelation.

What a blessing it was to be in Divinity School and to sit at the feet of some of God's best Theologians. Among them were Dean Clarence Newsome; Dr. Cain Hope Felder; Dr. Kortwright Davis; Dr. Alice Bellis; Dr. L. Charles Bennett; Dr. Cheryl Saunders; Dr. Evans Crawford; Dr. Gene Rice; and Dr. Delores Carpenter. What a joy to sit among some of God's best preachers and professors who were in the process with me. It was there that God truly showed me who God called me to be. The irony is that I was already walking in that calling, all my life, and didn't know it.

You remember my days started 3:00 a.m. One evening, I walked into one of my favorite classes with one of my favorite professors a few minutes late. One of my flaws is that I insist on arriving early wherever I go. But this night, for the first time, I entered the lecture late. I did my Director of Church Ministries duties; assisted with two funerals and a committal; helped several walk-ins, before and after the Homegoing celebrations; drove home to get the kids settled, fed and in the care of the sitter; and drove back to class. A bit vexed over what made me late in the first place (one of our regular street people who acted out), I attempted to be as non-disruptive as possible after I entered the lecture hall.. However, my beloved professor said something that really grated on my already frazzled nerves.,

He said, "Mrs. Miller! You are late! Dr. Hicks is not giving you your grade over here." That one statement was the tipping point. The camel's back broke.

I stopped in my tracks, only slightly turned to the right out of all due respect and said with a fatigued voice, "No Sir! You are exactly right, Sir. Dr. Hicks is not giving me a grade over here. You are not paying me a check over there. And neither one of you is taking care of home." I walked to my seat and sat down.

Maybe another day, I would have handled that statement better. My professor was not my opposition. In fact, he was extremely supportive of all students, and treated all students as intellectual equals, though he spoke and wrote like five languages at a time. None of my professors cut us any slack, though. That was absolutely as things should be. However, that cold evening was just one of those moments for him and for me. That night, I realized that the road to become an ordained preacher who is female, married with children was not well understood. Most of my sisters in seminary at the time were single. But, most definitely, I would not spend two seconds asking for understanding. No excuses. I respected everyone's journey.

God stretched me beyond what I thought I could bear. Unlike my Comrades who went to Seminary first, God literally worked me into my call, all in reverse. I received on-the-job training; and actually trained the male preachers who were brought on board on how to handle ministry on the ground, rather than from some lofty place. That thought kept me humble and oh so grateful. I would not spend one breath making an excuse for why I couldn't do what I was called to do. Besides, no-one would have heard me.

For me, I had to tow the line, just like my sisters in the military; and the women in ministry who were my professors. This was a time when women were just beginning to emerge as preachers in the Baptist denomination. We were still widely unaccepted. Women from other denominations were in Seminary with me which was great. Many watched my progress around the country, I learned later. Honestly, there was literally no time to notice what transpired. God threw me in the midst of a pivotal battle against the bastion of male dominance in the Baptist Church. Many men, clergy and non-clergy, and some women, were fortified against accepting women as preachers. Like our experience of being among 50 or so African Americans students at the University of Georgia, God quietly placed me in a fight for which I was unconscious of its impact or the providence of God.

There was no room, time or authorization from God to complain. That's what those who opposed preachers who are women wanted, so the role of women could be discredited. The goal was to get us to invalidate ourselves, the same method that was used to dismiss the Civil Rights of African Americans. Neither plan worked. The Church of Jesus Christ is the Body of Christ and the image of the Body was changing. The mandate from God was to get the work of Salvation done and represent Christ the King. Excuses did not count. They never do.

Ministry can never tolerate excuses. Daily, clergy traffic in the lives of people. Many people, real, alive people, are desperate to hear from God, and receive God's help through God's people who are clergy. Our missed opportunities to help people, cloaked in excuses of arrogance on one extreme or pettiness on the other, can be detrimental. No female whims or male machismo were or are ever permitted. Like my high school music teacher, Mr. Tranis Long, use to say, "Excuses only help the people who make them. They do nothing for the people to whom they are told." I love that. God is always up to something - to do God's best for us.

I was quite convinced that no one understood or had the time to be concerned about my situation. I was a preacher who is female and married with a family. No one can ever really understand another person's call or sacrifice for that call. We should share our experiences, an opportunity that was lacking for me. Compassion said to me that we can't walk in another person's shoes; but we can share the load.

Regarding that incident when I was chastised for being late or for any other reason, why bother getting frustrated when we are misunderstood. The Lord stretched me to that place I needed to be, that place where there was no way out. "I am here to learn", was the sign my Comrade Reverend Casey Kimbrough had over his door in his office when he was Director of Christian Discipleship at Metropolitan. I was in Seminary to learn, and in every spot where God placed me to learn. There is always a bigger picture. Myopic vision lacks spiritual insight and intellectual foresight. Spiritual Christian will see up close and far away.

God used even that otherwise insignificant moment with my greatly beloved, Biblically astute and highly esteemed professor for good. I learned at that moment that there was a rather large disconnect between the Academy and the Church that pretty much still exists, from what I can tell. What is taught in Seminary or Divinity School, and how the Church functions in service to the members and the community on a daily basis are very different situations. An invitation was extended to my beloved Professor and class members to go with our Street Ministries on a night jump to show love in ministry to the homeless. The Church and our members would give food, blankets, socks and a Word of hope to people sleeping on the street. Our class and professor accepted the invitation. Most had never had the privilege to witness in that manner. To be with them in that setting was such a profound moment. We were all blessed, including the people we served; so were our biological children who always went with me. We are blessed in unimaginable ways when we do the will of Jesus Christ without fear or selfish agendas

Through Howard's Divinity School, God stretched me to merge the intellect and the spirit to give birth to supernatural results. We must balance our personal lives and ministry. Too much Theology without application in the real world is a futile attempt to present Christ in a vacuum.

When God saves us and calls us, we are not told to leave our minds on the sidewalk on the way into the Church; or our spirits on the bench on our way into Seminary. None of us is all of that. All the pop-locking attitudes is a turn-off to people, and antithetical to the Biblical precepts of Jesus Christ. Balancing stretches us to see beyond our own vine and fig tree into the movement and power of God the Holy Spirit who decided, in the eternal past, to work through us for God's glory and our good. Real face to face ministry with the Anawim proved to my colleagues that ministry is not for cowards, but for the converted and committed Christians.

May I suggest to you that God stretches the mother-to-be from the inside out, beyond the limitations of the physical body, to enable the abdomen to accommodate the growing baby. Likewise, God stretches all of us beyond the barriers which the experiences of life erect in our spirits and minds. That stretching enables us to carry the supernatural things of God and bring them to the hour of birth. Some take physical form. As I think out loud, God stretched my state of consciousness to tear down the barriers that were imposed upon the most important areas of my life. Often, our obstacles are erected simply from what someone says and what we say about ourselves. God stretched me beyond my greatest obstacles that sounded like this.

.

- "You shouldn't ever get married."
- "You can't go to a white school (UGA) because you are Black."
- "You can never have children because your body is defective."
- "You can't preach because you are a woman."

One cannot really count the stretch marks of life. Obstacles may stretch us in ways that are a little more obvious. Rather, we should simply celebrate the fact that without our knowledge, God stretches us to make room in our lives for that which is Holy, divine, and ordained before the foundation of the world. Is it crazy to say that God stretches us beyond our limits? God stretches us to the limits of necessity. The stretching is necessary to remove self-imposed, human limits.

When a woman is pregnant, the Creator God has two humans utilizing the same space to process life, at the same time, with microscopic precision. That familiar statement of Christian faith that God will never put more on you than you can bear is precisely correct. Through the stretching process, God creates new pathways for us to understand more God, realizing we will never know all of it.

In the natural, a mother may actually go back to the pre-pregnancy dress size or even a smaller size once the baby is born.

However, it is most unlikely that the mother will ever go back to the same mental or spiritual state of existence that she had before she gave birth. For most mothers, the whole mentality and preoccupation with what is important really changes. Though our spiritual stretch marks are invisible, what God the Holy Spirit births through us changes us forever, as well. The birthing process supernaturally moves us to another place. Even women who may experience postpartum depression cannot deny that they were a participant in a major life moment that changes their lives forever.

Musings with God the Holy Spirit!

- Stretch marks are a testimony to the power and grace of Almighty God.
- Stretch marks remind us of how persistent God the Holy Spirit is to work a Miracle through us.
- Stretch marks remind us of the limitless power of Almighty God.
- Stretch marks remind us to keep confident of the Divine relationship we have with Almighty God.
- Stretch marks remind us of hoe God the Holy Spirit makes the impossible possible.
- Stretch marks remind us that there is life within us.
- Stretch marks remind us that there is life beyond us.
- Stretch marks remind us that our imperfections are made perfect through the blood of Jesus Christ.
- Stretch marks remind us that we are connected to the family of God.
- Bend1
- Don't break! STRETCH!!!

Chapter 12
Oh God!
You Made Me a Real Preacher!

I Timothy 4:14 - "Neglect not the Gift that is in thee, which was given thee by prophecy, with the laying on of the hands of the presbytery."

Thank you Almighty God. We graduated from the Howard University School of Divinity School Mother's Day weekend – Saturday, May 9, 1992. Friday, May 15th was my 41st birthday. The entire week after graduation, all day each day, including my birthday, was spent researching and writing a 50 page paper on Bible doctrine. This was the first time Pastor Hicks required that a Candidate for Ordination write such a paper. That long overdue service was scheduled for Sunday afternoon – May 17th at 5:00 p.m. In the midst of preparing papers and presentations for graduation, formal invitations to the Ordination Service, were sent to our beloved family, extended family, friends, Pastors (even those who did not approve), and my Professors to attend. God kept me oblivious to the fact that the Ordination was a significant event. Yet, I knew that all of my life moved toward that moment.

The Ordination Council would use the paper that I prepared as a part of the public catechism or interrogation. The Council could ask questions about anything in or pertaining to the Bible; extra Biblical texts; Bible history; Bible-based contemporary issues; and general questions about our Christian faith. The potential questions were unlimited. Once again, that was a change in the normal protocol. Dr. Hicks said that change was necessary to prevent the possibility of any challenge to my Ordination from anyone in days ahead because of my womanhood.

I understood and accepted that precaution which challenged me. We really did not know what might come up or who might rise up to oppose my Council or me. He said that if anyone ever questioned whether or not I was qualified, there would be more than sufficient evidence to validate my Ordination and my call. Trust me! There is. The evidence was videotaped in its entirety. I was only the second woman who was ordained at Metropolitan; among maybe a handful in the Baptist denomination in metropolitan Washington, at the time; and a precious few around the country.

My husband and our children, Atlanta family and extended family who came for the ceremony all went to worship service that morning. I could not, but rather remained in the hotel, where my parents were also. The hour seemed like it would never arrive, as I fasted and prayed from my cocoon. Ordination is the marker between God and the preacher to which the preacher will return quite often in the days and years to come. I sought the balance of God the Holy Spirit that I needed from my perpetual fetal position called prayer. The silence was all-consuming and comforting, as God the Holy Spirit centered me.

When we arrived at the Church that afternoon, the number of people who were there, an hour before the service, was unbelievable. Many of them, including the Deacons, Trustees, and staff had been there since the 7:45 a.m. service, which Pastor Hicks changed from 8:00 a.m. on the morning of my initial sermon. They ate breakfast and dinner there, and waited with precious enthusiasm for the service. A powerful "hum" was palpable in the atmosphere that could be detected; and generated the spirit of joy. Another Pentecost-type moment was present.

There was some concern about whether we would have a sufficient number of Ordained Baptist clergy to serve as the Ordination Council. I held my breath, as one by one, each of the distinctive Clergy entered. That was a monumental moment indeed. Reverend Dr. Christine Wiley was the only preacher who is a woman on the Ordination Council. How valiant Dr. Hicks, Metropolitan and the Council were to do what they did in the face of such opposition. There is absolutely no way for me to describe my gratitude to them, then or now, or ever. Thousands of times, over and over, I yet thank God for the way God worked the details. My Comrade, Reverend Patrick Young escorted me into the sanctuary. That blessed me.

Dr. Hicks was the Moderator who stood in the pulpit to call the session to order. The Council was robed in liturgical vestments. A sea of purple caught my eye as I entered the sanctuary. Those were my greatly beloved "Purple People" from our Victorious Christian Living Bible Class. Purple was the color of victory because of our Lord Christ and always our color of choice. Seeing them re-centered me to know that they were there. They lived through the entire process with me. I am forever grateful.

Everyone who I invited came - our Mothers and Father, brother, sisters, extended family from Atlanta; my Divinity School Professors and students; our Swinton Drive neighbors; and friends from Washington, Maryland and Virginia who did not attend our Church. The presence of the Metropolitan Baptist Church family was overwhelming. The sanctuary was filled with wonderful, incredible people who dared to own the moment. It was indeed a Holy Spirit empowered, ecclesiastical moment that each of us helped to make happen because of our faith in Jesus Christ. Our presence affirmed our belief that God does call women to preach. The presence and power of God the Holy Spirit reigned throughout the Church, and in each one of us.

They were all there - my husband and children, the people who I loved and people who loved me. But, I was all alone in a place where God resided alone with me. The moment was like the lifetime it would take to rear our children. The moment had to be seized. In my mind and spirit, there was only that moment to get it right. I dressed the part, for all women, in a pearl white suit and shoes from Nordstrom's. The skirt appropriately covered the knees. But, in reality, I was spiritually naked before the throne of God.

There was a sign that hang in my office from day one that said: "If you were accused of being a Christian, would there be enough evidence to find you guilty." The evidence had to always prove me guilty of being a Christian. At that moment, that day, I had to be found guilty of being a preacher who God called. My very soul was exposed. There was no fame, prestige or position attached to my call or commitment. I just wanted to be guilty as charged of being a preacher. The Council was not my enemy. They were charged with the responsibility to validate my call and readiness for service in the Gospel Ministry. Neither cordial discourse nor pleasantries had any place in the process that day. That day, I know that they wanted me to pass, but they could not or would not help me to do so. God the Holy Spirit directed them. I would not humiliate God's Grace through them. I stood.

Reverend H. Wesley Wiley was my Catechist. We worked together for weeks on the possible questions from the Council. What an enormous gift he and Mrs. Doris Wiley were to me and my ministry, and the ministry of countless others. At the time, he held the distinct honor of performing the service of Catechist for the greatest number of preachers in the Washington, Maryland and Virginia area. He was an unbelievably kind, well prepared, and humble servant who was a confidante, and wise, spiritual guide. Reverend Wiley posed the opening two questions.

All of my answers to every question suddenly took on the same format, something I had not previously considered. The answer to the first question was biographical and included my Christian experience. "What is your experience of call", was next.   I concisely stated the truth. Reverend Dr. L. Charles Bennett, my Homiletics professor, asked a question to which an appropriate response was given. Reverend Dr. Casey Kimbrough shocked me with his presence, and blessed me with his question. He took a flight to Washington immediately after the morning worship at Mount Carmel Baptist Church in Charlotte, North Carolina to be present. I didn't know he was there. Indeed, I was on the witness stand before Almighty God, the heavenly host and that assembly to defend my call and qualifications to preach the Gospel.

The Council asked important questions. I depended on direct assistance from God the Holy Spirit for every response. The answers were often accompanied with unprompted, thunderous applause from the congregation, which was out of order for the proceedings, according to tradition. I dared not show any emotion or reaction, neither did the Council.

After over an hour of inquisition and response, Dr. Bennett stood to make a motion that the Council suspend further interrogation. I was not sure if what I heard was what Dr. Bennett said. Essentially his motion was to end the questioning process. Reverend Wiley seconded the motion which was unanimously approved. He said that the answers were better than the questions. At that point, the house erupted in praise and we broke all protocol with shouts of thanksgiving. My Mother came to embrace me, a crucial hug, tears, and shout that I very much needed. Praise and tears flowed unrestrained, in all directions. Pastor Hicks subsequently joked that he had to catch me to finish the Ordination. Praise God.

The experience was a monumental, God-inspired moment for me, my family, and all who were present. My hair stylist and spiritual sister, Renee Harris, truly blessed me with a solo. The Chorus Choir and Male Chorus packed out the choir loft, and sang soul stirring music that raptured us. What a glorious, victorious day. The line of saints to present tributes and gifts was incredible. I owe them so much. God made what would have been an otherwise impossible situation possible through them. When it was time for the presbytery to lay hands on me, I felt the fire of God the Holy Spirit move through me like never before. The Shekinah Glory that hovered engulfed us. Only the power of God through the preachers kept me erect on my knees for the Laying On of Hands. I wanted that right. I needed that right.

God blessed me in so many ways, beyond my ability to articulate the generous grace of God. Over 20 years later, I learned that Dr. L. Charles Bennett was removed from one of the ministers' conferences because of his participation in my Ordination. I was and am greatly grieved at the thought. I never knew that until now. How arrogant and narrow minded were the attempts of that group of preachers to play God. That was the only way they could attempt their sly, slick and wicked protest.

From the depths of my soul, thank you Ordination Council for the boldness of Christ to ordain a woman in the Baptist denomination when you did. You opened the womb for more preachers who are women to be birthed. You gave life to my call. Rest in heavenly peace, Dr. L. Charles Bennett; Dr. H. Beecher

Hicks, Sr.; Dr. Maris P. May; and Reverend H. Wesley Wiley. The "preacher who happens to be a lady" loves you. You helped God change my life; and you strengthened me for the journey.

I tell young clergy that the process of Ordination is a special moment in time through which the preacher will remain grounded if we revisit that moment often. We wrap the mantle of Proclamation around the foot of the Cross of Calvary.

"Go Quickly and Tell!"

(Following is the sermon that Reverend Dr. H. Beecher Hicks, Jr. preached on the occasion of the Sacred Ordination of Nawanna Lewis Miller to the Gospel Ministry on the Seventeenth Day of May in the Year of Our Lord Nineteen Hundred and Ninety Two. The Reverend Dr. H. Beecher Hicks, Jr., was Senior Minister of the Metropolitan Baptist Church, 1225 R Street, N.W., Washington, District of Columbia.)

Matthew 28:7 – "And go quickly, and tell his disciples that he is risen from the dead; and, behold, he goeth before you into Galilee; there shall ye see him: lo, I have told you.

There are moments, distinct in every life, when God rocks your world! Strange as it may seem, it does appear that it is God's design, it is God's intent, it is God's purpose to rock our world. I don't know why, but now, after more than a quarter of a century preaching this gospel, I'm satisfied that God is in the rock business.

I've come to understand that not only does God rock your world, but God provides the rocks. God arranges the rocks. God has an agreement with the rocks. God orchestrates the rocks. God is in the rock business.   I do not know why, but it is so, that God will alter your path, realign your relationships, frustrate your family, disturb your peace, rob you of your sleep, interrupt your tranquility, intersect your serenity, change your assignment, redirect your mind, agitate your spirit, and send you off in a direction in which you had no intention to go. Like it or not, God is often determined to rock your world.

- God does not care who you are or what your personal plans or priorities may have been.
- God is not interested in your pre-designed career path development process.
- God is not interested in the petty matters of sex or gender.
- God's work is not confined to masculinity or femininity.
- God does not consult you or confer with you. And what is more…
- God does not require your wise counsel, your sage advice, or your considered judgment.

When the rocking sensation occurs, it is not your fault, nor is it the fault of any other. God is God. God reserves the right to be God. God does not need any help being God, nor does God require your input into the decision making process. The fundamental truth of your life and of my life is that God will rock your world.

Not only is it true that God will rock your world, but there are moments when God will put rocks **IN** your world. God has determined, or so it would seem, that those who are most committed to Him, will not go unhindered, unimpeded, or unmolested.

God has determined, or so it would seem, that on your journey you will be faced with mountains you cannot cross; and barriers you cannot break; and walls you cannot break. And, if no one else does it, God Himself will put rocks in your world.

Don't you find it a thing most strange that those who give their lives to the Lord will either find someone or something in the way? Once you begin on your journey with God and for God, I think you ought to know that rocks will be in your way.

- The rocks of hierarchy, history and traditions.
- The rocks of religious arrogance and Biblical ignorance.
- Rocks of ecclesiastical chicanery and theological sleight of hand.
- The rocks of egotistical elitism, spiritual sexism and baptized bigotry.
- The rocks of skeptical women and insecure men.
- The rocks of politics in the pulpit and jealousy in the pew.

Your degrees may be impressive in their order. Your academic standards may be saluted by scholars. Your preparation may be arduous and long. You may be "called", "anointed", and "appointed". But, I came to assure you today that God has fixed it so that without question, there will be rocks in your world.

This rock condition of which I speak is not new. It comes, as you know, out of the fullness of the revealed Word of God. The setting of this Word is familiar, Bible scholar that you are; and it will not take long to pass it in review.

The long crucible of Calvary has now come to its end. The long day's journey into night has come to its climax, amid the disturbing scene of midnight at midday, and of a moon dripping with blood. He who was born in a cradle has now been nailed to a cross. A crown was placed on his head. A spear wedged in his side. Vinegar was on his lips. Nails were in his hands.

A cry shivered up my spine when somebody heard Him say, "Father, into thy hands I commend my Spirit." The only thing left was for a Pharisee named Nicodemus and an undertaker named Joseph of Arimathea to come and to take down the body of Jesus, and place it in his tomb for burial. The long crucible of Calvary has now come to its end at the tomb.

Now, the scriptures tell us that when Jesus was buried, "a great stone" was placed in the door of the tomb. And, not only that, the guards came... the representatives of the Roman Imperial State... the guards came and sealed the stone and then watched it all night long. In fact, Matthew says "they went, and made the sepulcher sure, sealing the stone, and setting a watch."

- That's strange. No James. No Andrew. Just Mary Magdalene and the other Mary.
- That's strange. What happened to Philip and Nathaniel?
- The only ones I see are Mary Magdalene and the other Mary!
- That's mighty strange, I tell you. What happened to Thomas, and the Sons of Thunder, and Simon the Zealot?
- And whatever happened to Matthew himself who tells the story? You don't see anybody else, do you? Nobody here but Mary Magdalene and the other Mary!
- The Church ought to be alarmed that at the most critical point of the Church's history, there's nobody here but two women.
- The Ministers' Conference ought to be convened.
- Who gave these women authority to show up for service?
- The Board of Deacons needs to take a vote. After all, women ought to keep silence in Church, and somebody needs to tell them that women are forbidden to teach.
- Theological Seminaries need to alter their curriculum.

They are brash, and bold, and brazen. They are audacious, and arrogant, and assumptive. They have appeared without credentials. They have acted without consultation. They have moved into arenas for which they are genetically, and biologically, and intellectually unfit and unprepared. If Jesus had wanted women in His operation, He would have numbered them with the twelve. And yet, I'm still taking attendance and the only persons I see are Mary Magdalene and the other Mary.

And that's when it happened. That's when God rocked their world! They were already challenged by the presence and the reality of the rock at the tomb, but now God takes matters in His hands and rocks their world. Now, listen! This is what Matthew says:

"And behold, there was a great earthquake; for the Angel of
the Lord descended from heaven and came and rolled back
the stone from the door, and sat upon it." (28:2)

Here then, it seems to me, is a Word to the Church. God is in the **Earthquake Business** and, if nothing else, will shake you up. When the earth beneath your feet begins to tremble and quiver, it will shake you up. And, perhaps, that's what this earthquake is about for the Church. What all of this says is: **"There is an earthquake in the Church"**.

- When religion is stuck in the ruts of the ordinary, God x will shake up the Church.
- There is an earthquake in the Church.
- When the men of the Church are satisfied that they have all the answers, God sends an earthquake to provide a few more questions and shakes up the Church.
- While the Boards of the Church have gone back to the Board Rooms of the Church, and while they are having a meeting, and doing "business", and holding elections and

collecting "dues", God has some women who will go out to the cemeteries of life where the hard work is and it shakes up the Church.

While the men of the Church are asleep, nodding on sermons they've heard before, dreaming deceptive dreams about power they do not have and strength they will not use, God wakes up the women and shakes up the Church.

Matthew's word is not only about rocking one's world, and rocks in one's world; and it is not only about earthquakes and the shaking of the Church. There is a Word here that goes directly to women. There in that Garden Mary Magdalene and the other Mary had a conversation with that Angel and the record says that not only did his countenance change, but his raiment changed, and even the keepers of the cemetery "did shake, and became as dead men". (v.4)

Don't you think it strange that here on Easter (Resurrection) Sunday morning, even then God was faced with dead men in the Church. Still, Matthew says that the Angel spoke to the women and said to them, "FEAR NOT, YE: FOR I KNOW THAT YE SEEK JESUS, WHICH WAS CRUCIFIED". (v.5)

Perhaps, then, that is the Word for this hour: **"FEAR NOT!"** Yes! It is true that there are moments when God rocks your world. Yes! It is true that there are moments when God puts rocks **IN** in your world. Yes! It is true that there will be those hours when you must stand in a cemetery all by yourself. Yes! It is true that there will be earthquakes when everything around you appears to be lost. Yes! It is true that there will be those who will question your integrity; question your sincerity; question the authenticity of your call; but the Word from the graveyard is: **"FEAR NOT!"** After your Ordination will come opposition, but the Word is "**Fear Not!**"

- The price of your profession, and the price of public exposure, and the price of popularity is that you will be taken to the cross, but the word is **"Fear Not!"**
- When you leave here today, do not expect equality from the brethren. Expect darts and arrows; sneers and jeers.
- Expect "spiritual wickedness in high places". BUT, I keep on telling you, the word is "FEAR NOT".
- On the other hand, your greatest enemies will be from those in the Church who are of your same gender, but with God on your side, **"FEAR NOT!"**
- It will be the saved and the sanctified, the blood bought and the water washed who will scandalize your name and call you everything but a child of God.
- They will say that they do not like you, but they must respect you as long as you represent the truth; and as long as you preach the unadulterated Gospel of Jesus Christ. So, **"FEAR NOT!"**
- "God is our refuge and strength, a very present help in the time of trouble." **FEAR NOT!**
- "Therefore will not we fear, though the earth be removed, and though the mountains be carried into the midst of the sea."
- "When the wicked, even mine enemies and my foes come upon me to eat up my flesh," "I will fear no evil". **FEAR NOT!**
- "God hath not given us the spirit of fear; but of power, of love and of a sound mind." **FEAR NOT!**
- "There is no fear in love; but perfect love casteth out fear." **FEAR NOT!**
- "The Lord is my light and my salvation, whom shall I

174

fear? The Lord is the strength of my life of whom shall I be afraid?" **FEAR NOT!**

On the day of your Ordination, I came to tell you that **the Angel** said... my **Angel** said... your **Angel** said... **Heaven's Angel** said... **"Fear Not!"**

Well, now! I've come on this journey not simply because God rocks your world, but because of a Word of advice given to two women in a cemetery. Now, if you are willing to put up with the rocks, and if you can stand the earthquakes, and if you can live through the shaking up of the Church, the Angel has some advice for you. Said the Angel: **"GO QUICKLY, AND TELL HIS DISCIPLES THAT HE IS RISEN FROM THE DEAD..."** (v.7)

Go quickly! In other words, don't let anything stop you.

Go quickly! Do not let the Church or Church folk confine you. Soar to the intellectual and spiritual heights of which you are capable for which God has created and called you.

Go quickly! Don't be detained or deterred.

Go quickly! Let no man or woman despise or cause you to think that you must defend the authenticity of your calling.

Go quickly! And when you preach, do not lose your femininity. Accept none of this foolishness that makes you act like something you are not. God made you a woman. God called you as a woman, and God expects you to represent Him with all of your charm, and all of your grace and all of your dignity. Be a woman!

Go quickly! Life is not fair; but God is.

Go quickly! Don't stay in the cemetery of broken dreams.

Go quickly! Do not take up residence in the valley of

despair.

Go quickly! Do not be blinded by the tears of your own self-pity.

Go quickly! There is no time to waste, no time to delay.

Go quickly! There ought to be some urgency in your ministry.

Go quickly! There is work to be done.

- Disciples need to be directed.
- Sinners need to be converted.
- The lost need to be found.
- Believers must be baptized.
- The hungry must be fed.
- The social order must be rescued.
- The rejected must be redeemed.
- Lepers must be cleansed..
- Lepers must be cleansed.
- People with AIDS must be loved.
- Drug addicts must be liberated.
- Alcoholics must be sobered.
- Families must be saved.
- Children must be nurtured.
- The helpless must be helped.
- The hopeless must find hope.
- And the Gospel must be preached
- **GO QUICKLY!**

If God has called you, you can't stay here.
If God has laid His hands on you, don't be restricted by the confines of the structured Church.
If God has spoken to you in a midnight hour, and called you by your name...

...don't let anyone question your authority...

...don't let anyone tamper with your power...

...don't let anyone snatch your zeal...

...don't let anyone take your hope...

...don't let anyone rob you of your joy...

...don't let anyone steal your shout...

...don't let "nobody turn you around".

GO QUICKLY!

But! Don't just go! That's the trouble with too many preachers NOW. Just going and arriving nowhere.

- Don't just go - too many Shepherds have nothing to feed the sheep.
- Don't just go - get something before you go - you can't give away what you don't have.
- Don't just go -- and, don't try to march before you kneel.
- Don't just go. Do something when you get there!

That's why the Angel said: **"GO QUICKLY AND TELL HIS DISCIPLES THAT HE IS RISEN FROM THE DEAD."** I thought I ought to tell you, as you come to this high moment of your life, that the preaching of the Gospel is nothing at all if it is not about RESURRECTION. As a preacher, you must speak with prophetic voice, but tell men about the RESURRECTION.

- As a prophetess, you must speak to the frightening psychosis of our society, but tell men about the Resurrection.
- As a Herald of Heaven, you must speak of the reality of sin in a value-less society and a conscience-less culture, but tell men about the Resurrection.
- As a witness of God's redeeming love, you must minister to persons at every point of their need - pimps, and

pushers; heterosexuals and homosexuals and asexuals; gays and grays; junkies and addicts; abusers and molesters; the poor and the perverted; but whoever and whatever they are, tell men about the Resurrection.

As a proclaimer of the Gospel, you must speak the great Watchwords of our faith – sanctification, justification, salvation, redemption, grace, mercy, and love – but never forget to go by Calvary and that Cemetery on Sunday morning and tell men about RESURRECTION.

The preaching of the Gospel is but a command to tell men about this glorious thing called RESURRECTION. The disciples had a chance to tell it; but they stayed home. So, **YOU** tell it. God never leaves himself without a witness. So, you tell it. If these are silent, the rocks will cry out. So tell it. The redeemed of the Lord ought to say so. So, you tell it.

- The redeemed of the Lord ought to say so. So, you tell it.
- Tell His disciples that Ezekiel was right. Dead soldiers can stand on their feet.
- Tell His disciples that dead men like Lazarus can step out of their graves and live again.
- Tell His disciples that Undertakers can go home and hearses can turn around in the street.
- Tell His disciples that stinking corpses can be revived.
- Tell His disciples that death has lost her hold.
- Tell His disciples that He who was dead is now alive.
- Tell His disciples that there is nothing dead about Jesus.
- If you don't tell anything else, tell His disciples: **HE LIVES!**
- **He Lives! Do you know He lives? I'm so glad He lives!**

Well, I must leave you now. But, before I go, I must tell you that there is a reason God rocks your world. It may be hard to understand, but there is a reason why God puts rocks IN your world. It may be hard not to, but, there is a reason why God sends an Angel to say: **FEAR NOT!** It may be futile sometimes, but there is a reason why God commissions you to tell His disciples about this thing called Resurrection. And so, I look here again at this Word and this is what it says:

> "And go quickly, and tell his disciples that He is risen from
> the dead; and, behold, He goeth before you into Galilee; there
> shall ye see him: lo, I have told you!"   (v.7)

You see, the reason why God rocks your world, and puts rocks IN your world is in order that you will understand that YOU DON'T HAVE TO DO IT BY YOURSELF. Your education is wonderful. But, you don't have to do it by yourself. Your training has prepared you for battle. But, you don't have to do it by yourself. God has given you a discerning spirit. But you don't have to do it by yourself. God has given you organizational and communications gifts. But, you don't have to do it by yourself. God has given you a theological intellect and a soul that the Holy Ghost has set on fire. But, you don't have to do it by yourself. **"BEHOLD, HE GOETH BEFORE YOU...!"**

- The same God that opened up the Red Sea...He goeth before you.
- The same God that provided Manna by day and fire by night.... He goeth before you.
- The same God that opened Zachariah's fountain... He goeth before you.
- The same God who is Daniel's rock hewn out of a mountain... He goeth before you.
- The same God who is Jeremiah's Balm in Gilead... He

goeth before you.

- The same God who is Habakkuk's High Tower... He goeth before you.
- Mary's Baby, who is the Resurrected Lord and King... He goeth before you.
- The Matchless Lamb of God... He goeth before you.
- Your Help in ages past, your Hope for years to come... He goeth before you.

Don't you worry. Jesus will be a Friend when you are friendless. He is a Mother when you are motherless. He is a demon driver and a soul reviver. Jesus is A Rock in a weary land and a Shelter in the time of a storm. Don't you worry! He goeth before you!

But, the Angel didn't end there. He said: **"Lo, I have told you."** Don't you be surprised at what the Lord can do. Don't you be amazed at what the Lord can do with you. **"Lo, I have told you."** And just in case you don't understand what **"Lo, I have told you" means"**, it means **"I TOLD YOU SO!"**...

- When the Lord makes you a "real preacher", I told you so.
- When the Lord raises up friends for you, I told you so.
- When the Lord makes a way out of no way, I told you so.
- When the Lord opens doors that no man can shut, I told you so.
- When the Lord shuts doors that no man can open, I told you so.
- When the Lord takes your weakness and gives you His strength, I told you so.
- When the Lord takes your sadness and give you joy, I told you so.
- When the Lord takes your loneliness and becomes your

companion, I told you so.

- When the Lord sees your tears and wipes every tear from your eyes, I told you so.

(Paraphrased Conclusion)

The story is told of a woman who was a widow with five children. She worked her fingers to the bone on three jobs to provide for them after her husband died. After several years of hard work and sacrifice, she became ill and soon died, also. She left her 18 year old daughter to care for the younger siblings, alone.

Like her Mother before her, Emily took on three jobs and worked her fingers to the bone to care for her family. Like her Mother taught her, every Sunday, she made sure that her siblings were fed, dressed in the best that they had, which wasn't much, and sent them to church. Living in the most meager circumstances, such was her life for years. She never complained, even as her health began to fail. However, just after the youngest sibling graduated from high school, Emily became terminally ill.

The Pastor came to visit Emily and sat in a chair beside her bed. He took her by hand and held it in his. He saw the scars that were on her hands and arms. They struck his attention. He read scripture, talked to Emily, and prayed for her. When he finished, she shared what was on her heart. With tears streaming down her face she began to speak. Emily began to explain the sojourn of her years since her Father and Mother died. With strained breathing, she explained.

"I have missed being in church every Sunday the way I used to be. But I never stopped reading the Bible that use to be my Mama's before she left. I always studied God's Word and obeyed God's Commandments. The physical weariness from all the working and taking care of my brothers and sisters took its toll on me. My greatest concern now that the end is near is will I make it into heaven? Where will I spend eternity?"

With a heart filled full with compassion, knowing all the sacrifice Emily made to care for her parents until their death and her siblings after their Mother's death, the Pastor fought back his own tears. He sought revelation from the Lord. In the midst of his own pain for her, he wanted to say something that was true that would bring Emily comfort and peace. He simply said, "Just show God your scars."

Nawanna Lewis Miller, there is a scar on your hand. If my memory is correct, I believe it is on your right hand. As you have had to explain to so many, so many times, you burned it when you closed the oven door on it to keep your baby from getting burned. When you come to the end of your journey, weary of life and the battle is won; carrying the staff and the cross of redemption. He'll understand and say well done. Just show Him your scars. **GO QUICKLY AND TELL...I TOLD YOU SO!** **(Author's Note: Candidate was totally wiped out, spiritually and emotionally, as Dr. Hicks began to sing the following hymn.)**

- "If when you give the best of your service, Telling the world that the Savior has come. Be not dismayed, if men don't believe you. He'll understand, and say well done..."
- Misunderstood, the Savior of sinners, Hung on the cross, He was God's only son. Oh, here Him call, His Father in heaven, Let not my will, but thine be done.
- Oh when I come to the end of my journey, And the battle is won; Carrying the staff and the Cross of Redemption; He'll under and say, "Well done."

Chapter 13
Oh God!
Please! Be My Strength!

Isaiah 37:3 – "The children are come to the birth, and there is not strength to bring forth."

I embraced absolutely every single word and nuance of the powerful Ordination Sermon, as Dr. Hicks delivered it, in the power of God the Holy Spirit. The sermon was not only a message of victory in Christ Jesus for my journey to that point, but it was also one of trepidation for what was ahead, though I didn't know exactly what that was. In so many ways, the sermon was one of the most prophetic sermons I have ever received, personally. The words were not just prophetic concerning me, but all who would dare to receive the mantle for Proclamation of the Gospel. One portion in particular hit me in my spirit, soul, and body like a spear. Dr. Hicks said, "You can't stay here." That double-edged sword cut me - a lot. And, I quietly bled - a lot.

At that very moment, I knew what he said was so very painfully true. I absolutely knew that. I could not stay with what was comfortable, and familiar. God invested too much in me for me to remain in the same space. There was more that God birthed in the earth through me than just the preacher. I didn't know what that was, but in the back of my spirit, I knew the birth of the preacher was just the prelude to my new beginning. I just knew I couldn't stay, but I didn't want to go wherever it was that God sent me that I did not know about yet.

In the fall of 1992, after my Ordination in May of that year, God sent two of our Comrades, Reverend William E. Harris, Jr. and Reverend Patrick H. Young to serve Church congregations in Dayton, Ohio and New York City, respectively. Needless to say, I was devastated. What would normally be a four-person clergy team was down to two – the Senior Pastor and me. Even with the best support staff and volunteers in the world who we had with whom to work, we were challenged. I worked four positions, including my own and an administration position for a few months while the search was conducted for replacements.

The great gift God gave me, in the midst of my personal sadness, was the blessed opportunity to assist Pastor Hicks to Baptize converts. Every month, there were 20-30 candidates for Baptism. Physically and spiritually speaking, that was a totally God-sized, supernatural experience. The congregation was totally elated that Dr. Hicks permitted a preacher who is a woman to assist him to Baptize. That was a first that would expand. I had very closely observed the process at the Baptistry as a Deaconess. As I carefully covered women and girls coming out of the Baptistry, I gained valuable knowledge that prepared me for this opportunity. The candidates were happy that I assisted.

We took the taller and heavier people first to preserve strength. The congregation enthusiastically applauded, as we got the first man down, under the water, and back up, without a problem; and each candidate that followed after that. All the Baptisms flowed flawlessly. In the Spirit, I felt like we honored the Salvation of Jesus Christ, who never baptized anyone, and John the Baptist who prepared the way of the Lord, through the power of God the Holy Spirit. God's Grace permitted me to perform every ministry in the Church. Thank God that Dr. Hicks was open to the leading of God the Holy Spirit to let me do the work of which I never tired. There was never gender bias which demonstrated him to be considerably ahead of many other Baptist Clergy in the country.

Finally, all positions were filled. Pastor Hicks and I trained the new clergy and staff in all dimensions of Metropolitan's ministry, which was extensive. Reverend Keith Kitchen was chosen as the Assistant to the Pastor. Reverend Kelvin Turner was chosen as Youth Minister. Reverend Dr. Cheryl Price, the first preacher who is female that Dr. Hicks ordained, was chosen as Minister of Christian Discipleship.

God's familiar tug at my heart and mind increased. When God moves me to do something, I always feel like a huge steamroller is behind me. The feeling began to set in even more. That is that moment for me when everything within me is on spiritual and intellectual lockdown. Movement is required, and it must be hastened. At those times, I feel as though that mythical steamroller will smash me should I tarry. That feeling is huge.

Then, there is a moment that often creeps into my spirit that does not leave me alone. It is the moment when my mind flashes back to the day when Mr. Nelson Mandela made his State Visit to Washington, D.C. in 1990, after his release from prison. Dr. Hicks and Metropolitan were blessed to host the Ecumenical Worship Service and luncheon in his honor with members of Congress and national leaders in attendance. For me, the participation of our Children's and Youth Ministries in the historical event was vital. That was another first. The Church had more than 55 adult ministries and 25 ministries to children and youth. Mr. Mandela and the other distinguished guests were aware of God's grace on Metropolitan. That visit required many to facilitate; and the security of the U.S. Secret Service. That was a historical event.

The staff receiving line was formed to welcome this awe-inspiring man to the United States and to our Church. God gave me a prophetic Word of Knowledge through Mr. Mandela. I continuously remember that Word, and yet hold them closely in my heart. He said, "God will do great things through your ministry." My gratitude was warmly expressed and received; and I held on to those words as if they were some kind of prophetic guideposts. Like that day in the White House when Dr. Mays spoke into my life, I knew God spoke to me through the soon to be President of South Africa, Mr. Nelson Mandela. Those were the same words that Rev. H. Wesley Wiley uttered just days before I accepted my call to preach. I knew that all three men brought a Word to me from the Lord. That Word of Knowledge that Dr. Hicks gave, *"You can't stay here"* was the exit notice so I would move to the next assignment. I was on spiritual lockdown.

Obviously, Mr. Mandela and I never met before. There would have been no reason for him to remember me, if for any reason we had. However, in a flash of time, God changed my life through him. I learned later, that he was said to be also an INFJ personality like me. If the same personality type is true, that would explain for me the seemingly automatic connection on the supernatural level that day. One INFJ knows another one INFJ when you meet without saying a word. We were connected on a supernatural plain.

Memories of the encounter with the phenomenal Mr. Mandela, in combination with the following thought, rarely left my mind and spirit from that day. In a paraphrase of what God said to Abraham, God said to me: "Get up from your kindred and acquaintances and go to the land I will show you." The kindred and acquaintances about whom God the Holy Spirit spoke were all of the marvelously incredible people, of all ages, from all walks of life who had become our family at Church and in the Washington, Virginia, and Maryland communities. God fast-forwarded me to do a lifetime of ministry in seven years. God restored the years. God redeemed the time.

Eventually, God made it clearer that the place to which God sent us was home to Atlanta. I took what President Mandela said with me, wrapped as spiritual truth, and as a secret treasure. God answered the prayer I prayed for years, from the days when there was only George and me. God would take us back home to Atlanta when our children began to date and our aging parents needed us just as I prayed. Finally, I didn't make that request anymore, but rather became contented to do the Kingdom work where God planted us, at Metropolitan and in Spectrum Consulting, the management consulting business God gave George. I forgot the prayer. God remembered and very specifically ordered our steps.

During our sons' and daughter's spring break from school in 1993, our family went to Atlanta. For three days, my husband and I searched for a new home. After we viewed the twelfth home, we were about to choose that house on which to place a contract. God has a way of speaking to us personally, in a very specific manner. God speaks to me in Holy numbers and scriptures. Did you know that I am really bad with numbers and math? (Smile!)

As we stood in the parking lot of the subdivision's clubhouse, something marvelous happened. On that incredibly beautiful, clear spring day, with a blessedness and serenity surrounding us, I heard God say, "Look!" Ever so quickly, I turned around, not sure what I would see, but I knew God's voice'. There was the most glorious, unbelievable image of a majestic mountain. The prominent smoke-rise lifted from it, which is probably why I did not see the mountain when we look at the new homes.

To say God stunned me would be a major understatement of the facts. Shock and awe are slightly better. As I stood there breathless, I heard God speak one of my favorite passages of scriptures, from one of my favorite books in the Bible, literally uttered from the mountain. It was as if God took me into the Bible itself, back in time, to hear Caleb speak, first hand. Coming from the top of the mountain, as soon as I turned around, I heard the indescribable Voice say: "Now give me this mountain." (Joshua 14:12). Needless to say, I bent over in absolute amazement and gratitude to Almighty God. Then, I dropped to the ground in a most impromptu act of worship that rather startled our very competent realtor, Bob Ford. I knew without a shadow of doubt, that God chose our location. I knew we were home. We placed a contract on the house and returned to Fairfax with photos.

As the saints sing, "everything was moving by the power of God". We identified the fantastic, newly constructed home. My resignation would be effective June 15, 1993, thirteen months after Ordination. The next thing I had to do was to visit the doctor to schedule that female big one, the hysterectomy, before we moved. My heart, my mind, every part of my sense and sensibility missed my good friend Dr. Fabro, immensely. Since he was no longer there to guide me, I wanted the next best person.

So, when we returned home to Fairfax, God led me to search for Dr. Oliver Kreitmann. He was the doctor who assisted Dr. Fabro at the time of my out-of-body, near-death experience with our daughter Mikah. A perfect arrangement was made in heaven, and Dr. Kreitman was still in the very transitory Washington area. He totally remembered me, and that eventful day almost 10 years prior to our wonderful reunion. The whole out-of-body experience was a major topic of our initial visit. We reminisced on all the details of that delivery. After the examination, Dr.

Kreitmann informed me that it was indeed urgent that I have the surgery right away. Once more, the tumors read like a produce section in the grocery store.

The plan was set in motion. July 7, 1993 was the date the surgery was scheduled, after our son John's birthday on July 2nd. That date would give me time to recover before moving home to Atlanta in August. Our home in Fairfax went on the market. The first week in August was set as the closing date for the new home in Atlanta, before the start of school. The Church and the Victorious Christian Living Bible Class would be told one Sunday prior to my last Sunday. It would be too excruciatingly painful, emotionally for me to handle the long goodbye. There were so many people who I loved dearly, and who loved our family and me. The move did not go over well with our sons and daughter. They were devastated, and so was I. Everything was organized and timed perfectly, or so I thought. The assumption was made that because we believed that God directed us to return to Atlanta, and helped us to select our home, surely everything would be in order; and occur right on time. That was not exactly the way things would be.

Two weeks before the surgery, I went to the doctor's office for the pre-op examination, and to donate my own blood prior to the scheduled surgery. Ten years after the last birth, and almost a year to the day of Ordination, we had another astounding Miracle in progress. A new baby quietly coexisted, totally undetected, in the mineshaft of a womb with the tumors for four months. How?

Until four surprise pregnancies happened to me, it was always unbelievable to me in the past when I heard stories about women who said they didn't know they were pregnant. I learned and repented of that judgment. (Smile!) It is possible NOT to know. Our ministry work was huge. The pending transition was huge.

The staff transition was huge. Trapped between a state of absolute joy and utter anguish for the loved ones who we would leave behind when we moved, I totally missed the evidence of pregnancy, if there was any evidence. Everything pointed to the tumors misbehaving. I didn't know; probably also because I was told, pregnancy was not possible. AGAIN! Even though the doctors recommended surgery after the birth of each baby, there was never sufficient time or circumstance to have the hysterectomy. In hindsight, what would be the difference in recuperating from surgery and having a baby? The fact is that we were just never led to have the hysterectomy. It is written:

Luke 1:37 – "For with God nothing shall be impossible."

God's plan is perfect. Thank God for God's plan. Once the doctor told me that I was pregnant, the suit that I wore to his office no longer fit. Was that crazy or WHAT? Thankfully the jacket hid the skirt that couldn't be zipped, so I could get home. My big bag took care of hiding the rest. Family members and people who saw me before the doctor's visit could not believe what they saw after the doctor's visit, especially my husband. The pregnancy really was miraculous and most unbelievable. How was that possible? I only had a couple of weeks to my last Sunday; and the announcement would be made about our new baby at that time.

I am an empath who has to fiercely guard that characteristic of my personality in ministry. As painful as it was, the time of my departure arrived. Though Dr. Hicks very graciously offered me the opportunity, God led me to forego preaching a farewell sermon. Spiritually and physically, I could not filter through the enormous grief of leaving our Metropolitan family; or our extensive and well-loved DC/Maryland/Virginia family.

At the conclusion of each worship service, the Sunday before my departure from the staff, Pastor Hicks made the announcement that I was leaving the staff; and that Deacon-Trustee George Miller and I were having a baby. The announcement was met with a very hysterical, incredulous gasp which precipitated laughter and resounding applause. In an unpredictable way that only our amazing God could orchestrate, the news about our new baby somewhat eclipsed the news of my departure from the staff, and brought great laughter and joy to surround the otherwise sad news. The following Sunday, the going away continental breakfast after the 8:00 service, and the going away reception after the 11:00 a.m. service were top of the line, as usual. Our beloved Chef Freddie Underwood and the Culinary Arts Ministry catered both, and out-did themselves.

For the next five months, Dr. Kreitmann placed me on very strict bed-rest. Initially, we spent a lot of time in the emergency room because of very serious miscarriage threats. After one of a whole lot of such visits, God gave me a Word of Knowledge. "Drink Gatorade!" That instruction made sense because each time we went to the emergency room the doctors gave me saline solution. As a result of drinking the Gatorade, the contractions were calmed; and the never-ending pain was eased. What a difference 15 years made from the wine I had to drink with our first baby. So, the trips to the emergency room were greatly reduced.

I began to lose actual body weight at a rate of 5 or more pounds a week. The weight loss was drastic, and unexplainable. The only solution was for me to eat a lot of meals, nearly non-stop, which for me was difficult in the best of times. My husband and our three children took amazing care of me. Watching them do so was painful because I was accustomed to taking care of them. Instead of freezing wine this time, George froze Gatorade for me to drink all day. I was not exactly helpless, just fragile and I did not like that. Food was left on the nightstand and tray beside the bed for me to eat because even walking to the kitchen was challenging. The testimony was that this time, the three children who were never supposed to be born took care of me, as well, after school. God used them and their Dad to help save my life, and the life of our new baby. God's plan is always perfect. They encouraged me to hold on and work with God to bring the baby into our family.

Space does not permit me to tell you how hard I attempted, for months, to make the move to Atlanta go forward. The move was predicated on the sale of our Fairfax home that just would not sell. After a couple of months, it became apparent that we would not close on what we thought was the perfect home for us. That was a deflating reality. Because the emotional stress and physical struggle to leave home for showings became too much for me, my husband used wisdom and his authority as the head of our household to take the house off the market. I was far too weak to do anything, but wait out the unfolding script. Therefore, we did not close as scheduled in Atlanta. We were packed and ready to go. Everything in my mind and spirit shut down. Nothing made sense to me. Leaning to my own understanding was useless because I did not have any. I had to trust God, even for the next breath, and the life of our baby. Everything! Is not that what we are supposed to do anyway? I was flat out of choices.

Once again, the doctor warned us of the inherent dangers, and what could happen. Four for four, we heard the same scenario over and over, again. The huge irony is that as life grew within, my body became very frail. A pale, walking skeleton more accurately described my appearance. While it seemed I was doomed for the dust, God greatly increased my faith. I was then and am yet grateful for all the prayers that were prayed for me, and the scriptures that were studied prior to that hour of need. They literally saved my life when I arrived at the point that I could not read the Bible, or pray, or think with a sound mind. The feeling of mental derangement taunted me. God the Holy Spirit held onto my mind for me, so I wouldn't break, and I knew it.

Psalm 91 became the spiritual mantra and marker for me. At first, I would repeat the entire Psalm when God the Holy Spirit led me to repeat it out loud from memory or read it from the Bible. In the spirit, God took me to the "secret place". I literally felt safe there. I was alone during the day, and vulnerable to the forces of darkness that taunted me, non-stop. Any distractions from my own breathing, like a telephone ringing, or a horn blowing three blocks away, were just that – a startling distraction. Thanks be to God for the spiritual warfare training to which God the Holy Spirit called and prepared me. God's grace is indeed sufficient. Grace, mercy, and Psalm 91 were all I had to hold me in the path of delivery.

My breathing and thoughts were labored, so every breath and every thought had to be precisely and intentionally measured. God grafted Psalm 91 to my soul. That was a good thing because as time trudged along, I could not say that Psalm or think it or know it in its entirety anymore, or any of the scriptures that I had known previously. Just the act of taking in oxygen and releasing carbon dioxide became more and more difficult and shallow.

So, my daily diet for spiritual affirmation came down to reciting these few words: "He that dwelleth in the secret place of the Most High shall abide under the shadow of the Almighty." Eventually, I could only utter the first three words, "He that dwelleth" without difficulty. Those Words became a marker of my condition for me, and the location where I was, the secret place. Knowing that the secret place existed had to be sufficient. Understand! I found the "SECRET PLACE" for God and me. God the Holy Spirit gifts me so well to speak of it. It is written:

Isaiah 37:3b – "...for the children are come to the birth, and there is not strength to bring forth."

Though the context of the scripture was known and understood, it somehow became my report. That text became real and a description of my daily existence. All of my physical strength was gone. Daily, I talked to the baby, spirit-to-spirit, like God and I talked when I was in that high chair; and when God gave me revelation about John the Baptist that enabled me to accept my call. "You have to help Mommy get you here. I can't do it without God and you", I would say throughout the day when the pain became unbearable.

The real challenge for me was that I couldn't pray or think or process or anything, any longer. However, somehow, that was the most spiritual place in my life. That spiritual state was an altered state or the shock cocoon about which I teach. In that state, everything around you shuts down, and God takes you into the "secret" of Psalm 27. Just that thought that God has secrets to reveal to God's anointed made me want to withdraw to the Holiest of Holiest where God's silence is absolute.

The life threatening part for me and the baby was that there were so many tumors that were growing along with the baby that there was no space for the baby to move. When the enemy tried to convince me that something was wrong with the baby or the baby was gone, I talked to the baby more. Those conversations were spirit to spirit. I now know through the revelation of God the

Holy Spirit, that God led me to send all of my remaining energy to the baby from the inside. I will always believe that God literally redirected my thoughts and abilities from the normal things of life, so that all of my energy could be centrally located in the womb. All of my physical power and strength were gone. God the Holy Spirit is the strength we need to reproduce what God ordains. It is written:

Isaiah 66:9 - "Shall I bring to the birth, and not cause to bring forth saith the Lord: shall I cause to bring forth, and shut the womb? saith thy God."

God miraculously brought the baby, the Miller family and me through that challenge that should have ended my life, also. God is Grace. It is one thing to believe God will bring us out of impossible situations. A totally different measure of faith is required to believe God for a Miracle that is assigned to you when hope for a Miracle is all the hope you have left. I had to believe Isaiah 66:9. The Word of God became the living instrument within my body to perform the work to which the Word was sent.

God worked from the inside out. God's Word always works from the inside. Therein is the substance of faith activated. Isaiah 55:11 is true. God's Word accomplishes that to which it is sent. The word was sent to a baby and would not return void or empty handed. The Holy Word has power far beyond our knowledge and understanding. The body that is totally surrendered to God is the body that God totally empowers to receive Miracles. It is written:

Psalms 119:27 - "Make me understand the way of your precepts; so shall I meditate on your wondrous works."

What God brings to the birth, God delivers! God told me the baby would be born on Sunday. For whatever reason, I really wanted a Sunday birth for our last baby. Even though the date was medically different, on Sunday, December 5, 1993, God delivered a Miracle, a baby girl. We named her Victoria ChristiAnna Melissa Miller for my Bible Class, our Theology, and her great grandmother. Through God the Holy Spirit, we are always victorious. Faith in God always gives us the victory. I was 42 years old, and we were considered older parents. Victoria was born 15 years after our first son was born; 14 years after our second born son; and 10 years after the birth of our first daughter. The recovery was long because I went down so far in my health; but the blessing of our new Miracle baby was just as phenomenal as that of our other children. Thank God that her Grandmothers came from Atlanta to care for her. It is written:

Luke 13:11 – "And, behold, there was a woman which had a spirit of infirmity eighteen years, and was **bowed** together, and could in no wise lift up herself."

For almost four months before the birth, I was the woman in Luke 13:11 who was bowed with a spirit of infirmity and could not lift myself. After delivery, I couldn't stand up straight, so I walked bowed over for weeks like I was still pregnant. One day, as I walked down the hall to answer the door with the baby in my arms for whom I was bent, God said: "Stand UP!" Just like that, I stood up straight. The spirit of infirmity invaded my body; and I accepted that spirit for too long. It kept me in an unhealthy place after the birth of the baby. I rebuked the spirit of death that hovered every time we had a baby. If I stay too long with the thought, the praise of Almighty God takes over in every fiber of my being.

When we put our home back on the market in the spring, it sold in three (3) days to a family just like ours. I was not aligned with God's time for the blessing to occur. The house that God designed for us was not even under construction yet, when God directed us to the site. Through every precious yet formidable detail, God taught me not only must we line up with God's plan, but we must also line up with God's time. Kairos - God's Time - and plan are absolutely, perfectly connected in heaven, and likewise manifested in the earth.

God also reminded me that a female child is born with all the eggs she will ever have. It was amazing how years later; God showed me the spiritual connotation of that fact. I believe that the same way that God created women to carry the eggs from the time they are born as an infant, God likewise has spiritual eggs within each us, male and female, from birth, that God the Holy Spirit fertilizes and brings to life, as long as we live. Trust God. God brings forth in time, on time.

August 13, 1994 was our daughter Mikah's eleventh birthday. It was George's and my 22nd wedding anniversary. AND, we closed the door to the only home our four children had ever known in Fairfax, Virginia. We moved to Atlanta, one year after WE planned. God gave us a brand new house, in the same subdivision where we chose the first one. In fact, the second house was bigger, and perfectly configured to our needs at the time, and the future. God the Holy Spirit precisely arranged all of the details. The way our subdivision is configured, we can see the rear of the first home from the front porch of our home.

According to God's plan and time, we planted a non-denominational Church and Parachurch Ministries in the Deep

South. Years later, after our baby girl was born, God showed me how I would need her as a physical model of what God birthed spiritually through us. The birth and parenting of Victoria helped to make everything in ministry make sense. In other words, at the same time that I carried our baby, I also carried The Messiah's Temple Christian Ministries, The Institute for Christian Discipleship, Inc., Hannah's Hope Family Life Ministries, and other ministries that God brought into existence in the earth realm. God the Holy Spirit's Gift of Apostleship is and always has been fully active in my life. I made futile attempts to deny that Gift, too. Add that one to my sin of convenience.

As I watched our daughter grow through the years, I could see a tangible, physical model of how to birth ministry and nurture it to maturity. God knew I needed that so I could "see" how the ministries would look if they were a person. The same care and attention had to be given to the ministries as the human child. What God births through us is there in us from birth. God's time is God's. The ministries were there in the spiritual womb from the beginning. The Divine Majesty of God, our Creator and Lord, out distances any and all descriptions or approximations.

When I first heard the real live voice that I thought I heard when I would talk to Victoria before she was born, I was shaken. I would always say in difficult moments of physical pain, "You have to help God and Mommy to bring you in." I always sensed that she heard me, and that I heard her speak back to me. One day, out of the blue, in our kitchen while I was cooking, she got up to the counter on the step stool and said, "I will help you Mommy". To hear what she said and how she said it, rendered me speechless. That was the sound of the same voice and the same words that I heard from the womb. As strange or crazy as that sounds, the experience is true.

One day, I prepared to take a trip to Fellowship Missionary Baptist Church in Minneapolis to conduct a revival. The Pastor, Reverend Al Gallmon, is my Comrade. I never leave home without making sure the house is clean; and food is prepared for the family to eat each day that I am away. I ran around in a mad rush. All of a sudden, as I prepared to go to the airport, Victoria took my keys out of my hand, and stood there. I struggled to be patient, at that moment, to see what that was about. There was a tiny bottle of oil hanging from the bottom of my key ring. Baby girl took the oil bottle, and pretended to remove the top. She did as she had seen me do when I pray for people. She requested me to stoop down, and then she said, "I won't let you go until I bless you." WOW! She really blessed me. Those words were only a slight variation of the words that Jacob said to the angel with whom he wrestled, as described in Genesis 32:26. That was a moment. She was only three years old, but what a message. We must really battle to hold onto our spiritual selves. There is much that God transmits to the child that we often lose.

As I said during my Ordination Catechism, God is whoever we need God to be. God is boundless, without the limitations of humanity that we impose on God and ourselves. For me, God has always been Father. Even our death is not a limit to God. Therefore the range of God's strength is immeasurable.

Musings with the God Holy Spirit!

- Genesis 32:2 - "And he said, Let me go, for the day breaketh. And he said, I will not let thee go, except thou bless me."
- God blessed us with all spiritual blessings.

Chapter 14
Oh God!
They Say I Had a Veil!

Jeremiah 1:5 – "Before I formed thee in the belly I knew thee; and before thou camest forth out of the womb I sanctified thee, and I ordained thee a prophet unto the nations."

I was born with a veil over my face. Chances are that you have never heard of that phenomenon; or if you have, you probably know relatively little about it like me. To research the term has taken me over fifty years to finally even consider this subject, much less talk about it. Not even in my private moments did I ever dare to remotely think of this matter. Of all the things I would rather not talk about in this book, or ever, this one takes first place. The subject is brought up only because God leads me to think it through with God the Holy Spirit, for God's purpose.

What God reveals about the veil will help someone else to know and believe some divine Truth about God that God reveals. Most especially, those who grew up to believe the taboo about those born with a veil, will experience another dimension of the unlimited capacity of the Creator God. God urges me to accept that there is a spiritual revelation and connection that makes the veil real and relevant. I surrender to God. Clearly, there is a Word from the Lord regarding this little known fact of childbirth known as the Caul Birth or the Veil. God speaks. I have no authority either to embellish or to ignore what God desires to be said and written.

When I was young, around eight or nine years old, my Mother's first cousin, who was old enough to be my grandmother, told me about the day I was born. I have held onto that "hush-hush reveal", somewhere in my mind and spirit, all of these years, until now because I didn't know what to do with it. Clearly, it was not time to do anything with it at all until now. The Prophet Jeremiah of the Old Testament was so correct. God calls us and ordains the prophet before we are born. Romans 1:20 gives us the understanding that the invisible things or qualities of God are understood through what God created.

Down south, specifically in Atlanta, Georgia where I was born, long before most of us had one much less two cars, or a driveway, or a two-car garage to put them in, we always walked each other home. One of the rituals of goodbye I call "peace the way home". They meant "piece" or a portion of the way home. But, as God has grown me through the years, and the older family members have left one by one to go live with God, the spelling has changed for me. I once preached a sermon using that subject. The ritual is based on what friends and family consented to do when anyone came to visit. Visit they did. Time and reflection insist that we spell it the other way. The backdrop of our family experience is shared, so that you will understand the context of the revelation..

There was always plenty of food in our house, laughter and courtesies extraordinaire. Preachers and Church Class Leaders from Centenary Methodist Church, our Grandmother's Church, and Flipper Temple A.M.E. Church, our Mother's Church, Church members and relatives always made their way to our table. All of them would dress up for the visits like they were going somewhere really important. They were people who always looked important and very distinguished to me as a kid. I learned to spell that word "distinguished" early on because of them. Someone said it once. I looked it up in the dictionary. Distinguished became a frame of reference for me early in life.

One relative in particular, Cousin Willie, who owned his own barbershop, over by Morehouse, comes vividly to mind. He always dressed in his best suit of many; wore his best ties; and his lint free fedora. His white handkerchief was always folded just right, and placed in the front of his jacket. He always had one handkerchief in his jacket pocket and one in his pants pocket to wipe the familiar sweat. He usually came on Mondays when beauty shops and barber shops were closed. The Pastor of our Grandmother's Church was also, always, a frequent visitor. A spread was always set for him, too, as it was for everyone, every day, even when it was just us. The Class Leader from our Mother's church made frequent visits to pick up the offering or just to check on our Mother and family if she did not make it to Church.

For most of my early years, our family included five children, our Daddy, Mother and Maternal Grandmother. Unlike many who tell similar stories of the old South, Mama didn't give the guests the best pieces of chicken. She only cooked and served the best pieces for everyone. Mama always cooked two meats, vegetables, a variety of homemade bread and desserts, every day, even when she went to work. There was always more than enough to share with "pop callers" who were many. Her children always ate first. That was her rule, and definitely our Dad's.

Daddy often did more tolerating of the visitors than communicating, if he were home and not working. Though he was more than generous, a lot of small talk was not his favorite thing to do. He was always gracious and very generous, though short on the chit-chat. He did not really have social occasions, just community service and activism. Daddy worked very hard to make sure all of us ate well and often, including people in the neighborhood. When I got older, I often told the story about how on Sunday, I would strategize to inconspicuously run ahead of people who may have followed us home from Church to make sure that I got ahead of the crowd for dinner. It did not matter. There was always enough food.

When the time of departures was at hand, we walked our guests halfway or peace-the-way-home as we called it, usually with our Grandmother. Then, we would all pause at the halfway point. The adults would talk some more. Then, the cousins would in turn, walk us peace-the-way back, covering terrain we had already walked. This could have three or four segments of such behavior of love in a single trip.   The adults talked about everything in a rather lofty manner. The common belief was that God would make things better for us "d'rectly", meaning eventually or before too long.

As children, we tagged along with the adults. We were seen but not heard, except maybe me. (I have to laugh at myself right here.) The rule was that we were to be on our best behavior at all times, everyone. The adults did not speak in our presence about anything that we couldn't hear, but rather they spoke mostly about God, what God had done or would do, and family history. They were great Christian ladies and gentlemen.

With that back drop, I remember one occasion when I walked one of our older cousins "peace-the-way home" without anyone else one day - alone. For whatever reason, she decided that was the best moment to tell me what appeared to be one of those hush-hush family things about which no one talked. For example, using the very word "pregnant" was against the social order in our family, back in the day. So anything that pertained to "that" word was strictly off limits. As a matter of fact, if their souls and spirits were not all in heaven, they would turn over in their graves and get up if they read what I share in this book. Smile!

As the cousin and I walked, we made small talk that I disliked as much as my Daddy disliked it, eve then. Suddenly, out of the blue, without any connection or provocation to anything to which I could relate, my cousin said, "You know you were born with a veil over your little face." I didn't get that. What does that mean, I mused. As a young child, I thought the Veil was like the one that women wore on Church hats back then or when a close relative passed. She seemed to wait for a reaction, except I did not know that to which I should react. Though I sensed that I should say something, I didn't. According to her, that little fact was something that no one wanted me to know.

Our Mother's dear, sainted first cousin, who was significantly older than Mama, seemed as if she felt duty-bound to tell me the family secret. I accepted that she told me. At the time, the question in my mind was more why SHE felt the need to inform me, if I was not supposed to know, since I had not a clue what she meant. I never responded to my elder cousin. In my mind, it would not have been proper to do so. That was all she said because that was all I wanted to hear from her about that mystery subject. So, we pretty much walked the rest of the way in silence. If there was more that I should hear, I wanted my Mother to tell me. I think I felt kind of sad or afraid that my Mother had to deal with the repercussions of whatever that was that I did not know.

Despite being the brazen child that I was, I waited a few days before I asked my Mother about what her cousin said. My Mother was quite upset that I was told, but confirmed that what our cousin said was true. Yet, she attempted to explain and play the truth off, at the same time. The limited information that Mama conveyed seemed rather harmless, but somehow very serious or personal at a level that was too much for her to repeat. I presumed a great deal from her struggle to tell me what happened. I felt sad that whatever the Veil meant caused her so much difficulty. She repeatedly said that day, and afterwards, "You were different". I couldn't understand why until now. Who, especially a child, would want to be that "different" – whatever that difference was? In the back of my mind, I knew that she was afraid for me, so we never talked about her secret anymore. We kept the "knowing" to ourselves. God the Holy Spirit prompts me, now. It has taken this long for me to reconsider that day, and revealed though limited information, about my birth. Clearly, God prompts me.

Simply stated, according to what God led me to research, babies who are born with a portion sack are called Caul Births. The Caul (scientific description) is also known as the Veil, the Veil of Tears, mantle, or helmeted head in common descriptions. The Caul is a fetal membrane that tightly covers the head and face of a baby at birth. There is a range for the presence of the Caul, from the partial presentation of the membrane that covers the head and face, to the birth of the baby in the full amniotic sac that is not broken in the normal birthing process. That is defined as "En-Caul". With the En Caul, the baby does not realize it has been born yet because it is still in-cased in the full amniotic sac. The baby continues to behave as if she or he is still in the womb. Both forms of Caul births have inherent dangers attached to the very survival of the baby.

The term Caul means, "**born behind the veil**". Babies who are born with the Caul or Veil are called Caul Bearers. Caul births have always been rare. Current statistics list their number at less than 1/80,000 births. According to folklore and legend, a baby who is born with the Caul or Veil has special insight and unique abilities. In some cultures, the Caul or Veil has great religious significance, both for good and for evil. Some cultures treat it as sacred. Others cultures treat it as a good luck charm. Some purchase the Caul for the purpose of securing luck, especially for sailors. Still others developed strange superstitions and fears regarding the Caul. I wonder how much of that truth, history, and folklore or superstition was transferred to my Mother

Throughout history it seems, cults have formed around and because of the Caul. As information regarding the rare birth is finally gaining interest and momentum, there is more evidence on the Internet, and in periodicals. Much of the information portrays the occult-like, dark side examples pertaining to this phenomenon of birth that still has no real explanation for its occurrence. God has a purpose for Caul births.

Even now as I write, I want to back away from any discussion about the Caul or Veil. However, God the Holy Spirit moves me forward. Literally, my point of discovery is in real time for this book and not historical, as most of this book is written. God does all things perfectly, in God's own time – God's Kairos.

While some would say the content of the following description is subjective and not scientific data, the article very accurately speaks from the viewpoint of the Caul Bearer who wrote it. Likewise, most of the words contained the description reflect many of my own, personal experiences. Gratitude is expressed to Shannon Lee Wolf, Founder of Caul Bearers, for her permission to include the description and the website that gives valuable insight. The description better explains me to me, and me to you. I may more adequately transmit my thoughts about what all of this means, as God the Holy Spirit gives me direction and insight.

For sure, I finally make even more sense to me, if to no one else. I researched Caul Births and write from the perspective of a Christian to hear what God says.

We seek to dispel anyone's attempt to suggest that the description that follows is self-serving in some way. Please let me hasten to say that the burden of living with the reality of the Caul is too great to even want to acknowledge the Caul, much less trifle with it for selfish gain. That was true, even when I didn't know what I know now. Most people who were born with the Caul or Veil would probably say they would not have chosen this birth for themselves, if it were their choice. God does not ask our permission. Rather, I personally seek answers from God the Holy Spirit and from other Caul Bearers to benefit God's Kingdom. I am confident that this rare birth has Kingdom significance. The visible reality permits us to understand the invisible reality.

Please know as you read the following description that I am a Born-again Christian. Some of the terms used do not relate to my system of belief or me. However, I respect the truth and value the authenticity of the description Shannon Lee Wolf gives. Therefore, I incorporate the description here. We flatly refuse to major in minors.

"What Makes Caul Bearers Different?"
Shannon Lee Wolf, Founder of Caul Bearer
http://whatisacaulbearer.webs.com/aboutcaulbearers.htm

"Caul Bearers are vital human beings to the growth and insight of humanity. What they see, hear, and feel, tells tales of things to come, things from the past, and things we all need to know. They are messengers who are in touch with the world beyond the physical plane. They are sensitives, visionaries, shamans, mediums, and healers, writers, actors, poets, and artists. Each has their own unique gifts to share with the world, and yet the unnerving presence of a Caul Bearer tends to repel the very people who need them the most."

"Most Caul Bearers are "truth tellers", with the tendency to blurt out the silent, lurking evidence of the "elephant in the room", with casual abandon. Caul Bearers are mirrors for others, and so often are misunderstood as being a person's hidden dark side... which of course leads to various types of abuses and rejections."

"Caul Bearers see ghosts and other entities, hear voices, remember their past lives, and have visions of the future. Such flashes come without warning -- in "day dreams" or night dreams, and can be horrifying or blissful. But, in the long run, being a Caul Bearer is a heavy burden to bear, and most have experienced or have issues with addictions to ease the pain. Many have thoughts of, or have attempted suicide as the only means of escaping a life of perpetual torment. Some are misdiagnosed as schizophrenics and are heavily medicated. Most are inclined to be solitary creatures and avoid crowds."

How immeasurably insightful, inspiring, and helpful for me is that description of Caul Bearers. I am extremely grateful to Sharon for the work she does for Caul Bearers. I could literally check almost every box, if it were formatted as a list. Integrating all of those truths to form a "normal" existence was and is the challenge for Caul Bearers, including me. Now that I am able to process my thoughts and memory, God inspires me and I write.

Coincidentally or not, that day was the last time I remember that I walked our cousin peace-the-way home. Somehow, all those "peace-the-way-home" episodes in our lives culminated into that one. In a real way, that walk may be the best walk I ever took, in view of the revelation. Many years later, my spirit and thoughts are brought under subjection to the will of God and the divine lead of God the Holy Spirit to seek knowledge, wisdom and understanding from God about this birth phenomenon. When I said that I finally make better sense to me, I meant that. Let me give you an example.

I repeat and further explain that my first memory of God is when I was yet in a high chair. I remember that day with vivid clarity of details. My first teeth (more than one) broke through when I was nine months old. It was some time after that about which I can still see the room; still smell the scents; and hear the laughter. I took the old-fashioned wood match from the counter, as Mama and her sister, who was visiting with her family from Detroit, talked and made breakfast in the kitchen.

How the match was struck, I will never know. I know I struck it, but I don't know how I was physically able to do so. But, children have been known to strike matches and set houses on fire. It was summertime in Atlanta. I burned my bare chest with the match. All of a sudden, though easy and non-disruptive or threatening, the Presence that I now know to be God, appeared like a gentle parent in the room, up close and personal. I knew God and God knew me. That "knowing" of God the Holy Spirit still informs me, and has informed me even when I didn't know.

God gently disciplined me with His eyes, only, like a loving Father, as He blew out the match, all in an instance. That feeling of God's love, ever-protecting, ever-abiding, was indescribable, as I have reflected over the years. God had no physical form, just Presence. God never spoke, but I understood the secret was between us; and that I was to cover the tiny place where I was burned. God protected me. Mama never saw the burn. That event makes sense to me, now, in the context of the Caul or Veil. From the beginning, God was always there. I would see that same presentation of God as I prepared to accept the call.

All of my life, as early as I can remember, I heard someone call my name. Regardless of where I was, or what I was doing, I heard someone call my name. Sometimes, when I walked the long-distance home from school, I would hear my name called. I remember hearing my name one day as I walked home from kindergarten with my friend. Her Mother normally met up with us before we arrived where we were this particular day. The "Voice" said, "The bus is coming. Get out of the street." I did and I told my friend to do the same. She could not hear the bus or see it. Neither could I, but I got out of the street, and kept urging her to come walk on the grass with me. But, she kept playing in the street. Suddenly, out of nowhere, the bus speeded off the hill, brushed her, and she fell down into a deeply sloped yard. The bus driver came to a stop and ran back to her. God willed her to live.

I ran like the wind, faster than I ever thought I could run to get her Mother, who seemed to be so very far away from us that day. She and I ran back to the site, and saw her lying in the ditch. I just held on to something in my head and heart, but I didn't know it to be prayer or faith at five and a half years old. They put my friend in the ambulance and took her away. Petrified, I walked home alone, but not alone. God was there. My friend lived and we were reconnected in high school. That memory, and so many others like it, also helps me make sense to myself after all of those years.

The memories that lightning struck me twice are vivid to this day. The effects of those occurrences and others were so strong that I began to think something was wrong with me, or that I attracted evil to myself. When I was around six, I stood in the screened doorway, at home, when we lived in Detroit, to watch the beauty of the torrential rain, as it hammered down that summer day. Without warning, a bolt of lightning struck the metal jug that was used to prop the wood door open. I was knocked to the floor; and could feel the electricity go through my body. That instance was chalked up to my disobedience. God and I kept the secret, also, that I was where I was not supposed to be.

On another stormy, rainy, Georgia day, the thunder roared and the lightening flashed with what seemed to be malice intent. My sisters and I were home alone when lightning struck the telephone poll, and knocked live wires down. Some were stretched across the street. I got up from my quiet place with my sisters, and ran downstairs to make an emergency phone call to the operator to report the downed wires. Our parents would be coming home soon, and I did not want them or anyone else to be electrocuted crossing the live wire. As I attempted to get the operator to understand the emergency, lightening hit the receiver, and literally knocked me across the room. After a few minutes, I was able to think again. Still feeling the tingling in my body, I hung the telephone up and went back upstairs. I prayed for my parents and everyone, that they would not be hurt..

When I was around twelve or thirteen years old, I walked the long distance home from youth choir rehearsal at Church, rather than wait for the bus. There was an elderly lady with what looked like two heavy shopping bags who struggled to walk just ahead of me. I ran to catch up with her, and offered to carry her bags to her porch, which was on the same street. As I walked ahead of the woman carrying the heavy bags for her, a car hit the telephone pole behind me, and caused a wire to snap. With bags and all, I took off running, as fire popped from the falling power line. Clearly, that was a dramatic moment, as God gave me the strength to carry the bags and out-run sure disaster, at the same time. The bags were gently placed on the front porch, as we agreed, and I continued my eventful journey home. But, I was more grateful each time that God protected me. Like the match, I kept those events and their details between God and me.

In 1961, I was 10 years old when I watched the desegregation (not yet integration) of the University of Georgia (UGA) with my Dad on the evening news. We watched most of the events of the Civil Rights Movement, as they happened. That news included the terrifying riots, and the devastation of the Vietnam War, through the eyes of Walter Cronkite, Chet Huntley, and David Brinkley. Where possible, Daddy was literally on the scene. That day, God led me to declare I would attend that school with one simple affirmation. I declared to myself, "I am going to that college". I knew nothing about the school; or that I had to pay money to attend; or that it was in Athens, Georgia. Later, though accepted at other colleges and universities, I just knew I was supposed to attend UGA.

Just a short eight years later, I was there at UGA. Upon arrival as a starry eyed freshman in the fall of 1969, the first in my family to go to college, I was soon devastated. There were 20,000 students. Significantly, far less than 50, more like 25, were African Americans. Anticipation soon turned to abusive isolation and mental anguish. No matter how hard I attempted to fit in, I did not, or would not, nor could not fit in. We were treated as trespassers. I said 50 students, knowing that is an exaggeration.

So many days, as I walked the enormous campus alone, though in the midst of rather large crowds, I saw what looked like a group of African American students talking in the distance. I would break into a sprint to catch them before they dispersed. When I got to where they were supposed to be standing, they were not there. Why didn't I stop running towards those images sooner, like after the first time? In my eyes and head, they were so real that they had to be what I saw. They were not. They were something else. I now know that they were angels. I now know they were my protection and reassurance of some kind in preparation for my future ministry. I now know that I was seeing in another dimension. Astrophysicists say there are at least eleven dimensions, you know. I continued to see the angels, especially in dangerous situations, I just did not run to them anymore. There were times when my life was in danger when I am sure the angels helped me. I make sense to me, now, regarding the Veil.

The following fall semester of 1970, Dwight Thomas appointed me as the Mistress of Cultural Affairs for the Black Student Union (BSU). We had nothing on campus to which we could relate or in which to participate, as Black students, except the BSU. We were not welcome on campus, in the classroom, or organizations. Some faculty and students blatantly discriminated against us, while most of the students and faculty ignored us, at best. A precious few walked with us, despite their contemporaries. At night, someone put broken glass outside our doors for us to step on in the middle of the night if we had to go to the bathroom. Still other students rode huge horses to intimidate us especially during homecoming and old south days. Some attempted to trample us. Some used their fast luxury cars to threaten us, as they revved up the engines beside us. We were emotionally abused, but determined to succeed..

The first Black scholarship athlete, Ronnie Hogue, came in the fall of 1969, with the other nine students who were in our class. Hogue was an outstanding basketball player from Washington, D.C. He had to be or he never would have made it to Georgia. He was a star basketball player and our friend. The Black students were not just students. Our role as African Americans was to raise the consciousness level; help eliminate some of the problems in discrimination during our tenure there as students; and demand our rights. So, we protested for more Black students equal to the percentage of African Americans in the state of Georgia; Black faculty because there was none; and the addition of an African American Studies curriculum, among other things. We bore the mantle to effect change. Only if you were there will you understand the burden. All of that predates the Call, or does it? Was that mission, in fact, the prelude to it? We were a cause. We had to exceed our white classmates academically to acquire admission.

Alone in Creswell Hall, God gave me the vision for Pamoja Choir; Pamoja Dance Group; Pamoja Drama Group; and the Journalism Association for Minorities (JAM), which started Pamoja Newspaper. Talking about branding? The vision for all of it came straight from the Lord to me, the same way God gave me all the ministry answers, since then. The relationship to my later years in ministry is remarkable. The thought, even now, warms my heart. Dwight Thomas and the BSU instituted everything as proposed, like Pastor Hicks did for Youth Ministries, and Church-Wide Ministries. My gifts did make room for me then, according to Proverbs 18:16, at UGA; at Metropolitan; and all along the journey. We were still only a handful of African Americans, but we were intelligent and creative. The pressure of racism was enormous. For me, faith in God was greater. God's plan is outrageously blessed.

The Pamoja Choir became the African American Choral Ensemble (AACE); and was added to the UGA curriculum in 1988, eighteen (18) years after God first gave me the vision. Thousands of students of all races have been a part of AACE through the leadership of Dr. Sharon Willis and Dr. Gregory Broughton. At this writing, Dr. Broughton celebrates nearly 30 years of phenomenal leadership. At his 25th anniversary celebration concert, he, AACE and UGA graciously presented me with an award, as the founder of Pamoja. At the time, when God gave me the vision for the choir and the other components, I did not have the slightest idea what I was doing; and knew nothing about branding. I wholly honor God, the revelation of the vision, and what God permitted. God led me through. Forever, I will be grateful to my beloved brother Randy Groomes who is currently Director of the Office of Diversity in the Terry School of Business. He is a UGA graduate of UGA. I thank God for the excellence of Randy, Dr. Broughton, and others on the faculty and staff. They bring some fulfillment of the vision of the early African American students. We are UGA, too; I can finally say.

God the Holy Spirit led me to understand that everything was to be Pamoja to lay a plank in the bridge to begin to cross the cultural divide between the races. I now know that God used me to do something and taught me something I didn't understand. God put me between the very massive rock and the very hard place at UGA to form the preacher. God presses from us all that God has placed in us for God's purpose, at the time God predetermined for the pressing. Though strong relationships were developed at UGA, I now know also that the experience of extreme isolation was characteristic of the Caul birth. The racism was real and prompted me to finish in three and a half years, taking over 20 hours each semester to do so. There was never any reason to go back until now.

In defense of my Caul, Birth, at the risk of sounding like a total crackpot (smile!), let me hasten to say this. Yes, I have seen dead people, too. The first time was in the third or fourth grade when I frequently saw my Dad's deceased brother, Uncle Douglas, who Daddy loved with a big brother's kind of love for his baby brother. The first time I saw my Daddy cry was when Uncle Douglas died. When I saw him, I figured he was there to protect us. I was not afraid.

The second person that was revealed to me, more than once, was a woman who sang in the choir at our church who was deceased. I was always early for Angels of Glory Children's Choir rehearsal on Thursdays at 4:00 p.m. Though I never saw the lady alive in person, when I went to choir rehearsal she was seated on the front row in her choir robe. When I described the lady to my Mother, she knew exactly who the woman was. When I told Mama where the woman was sitting in the choir loft, Mama said that was the seat she that she occupied while alive, when they sang together in Choir No. 2.

The third person that I saw who left a lasting impression was my cousin's husband's first wife. His former wife was also deceased. I described the woman to some of my other cousins in very vivid details, after I encountered her. The woman sat in a rocking chair in the room where George and I attempted to sleep. Needless to say, I did not sleep at all that night. I just watched her, as she watched me. I kept waking George to ask him if he saw her. Like the supportive spouse that he is, he said he did, but I am not sure. The ice and snow on the ground seemed to grind time to a halt that night. Because of her presence, I was frozen in place until the morning sunrise which seemed as if it would never occur.

There is insufficient space to recall all the Miracles, signs, and wonders that God the Holy Spirit permitted and yet permits me to witness in my own life. I am reminded that there are no bragging rights in Christianity. Neither does God the Holy Spirit permit us to place our light under a bushel or hide who we are as the city that is set on a hill. It is written:

Hebrews 2:4 – God also bearing them witness, both with signs and wonders, and with divers miracles, and Gifts of the Holy Ghost, according to His own will."

Consistent with elements of the Caul Bearer, it is normal for Caul Bearers to see through the natural realm into the supernatural realm of the Spirit. That characteristic is difficult for many to understand because no one of whom I am aware has sufficiently explained the power of God that is resident in people who were "Born Behind the Veil" or Caul births. That is why I believe there is greater significance that God reveals through this book. God said it and Christians must really believe that all things visible have an invisible parallel, according to the Holy Bible. Will the born again daughters and sons of God begin to believe, En masse, in the powers of God the Holy Spirit to work in us and through us, in the Spirit realm, to impact our natural reality?

A reference point, as a Caul Bearer or person born with the Veil, would have been so helpful to me, if I had known, what I know now, when I was younger. But, could I have handled the information at an earlier point in life? I didn't even know that I should pay attention to this little known, but significant, though peculiar, circumstance of birth.   I did not know anything about the Caul or the Veil until now. The God of Jesus Christ protected me. I now know the danger that lurked around me to prevent this moment. As Genesis 1:1 records, "In the beginning God created the heavens and the earth." The vastness of the physical creation is yet to be discovered. In terms of spiritual revelation and exposure to knowledge, God has even more infinite details to reveal.

"The Otherness" of God is discovered, as God reveals different aspects of creation, God's will, and who God is to us. Therefore, I search and seek the thoughts of the Triune God to find answers that make the Caul or the Veil relevant to all believers. God gives us what we need, including what we need to know, when we need to know truth. From the beginning, God protected my mind and my life. Just because we either do not see, or we do not understand, or we refuse to learn about the "Otherness of God" does not mean that "Otherness" does not exist. God has different configurations of the universe, and our relationships to those configurations that have yet to be discovered. Astrophysicists say there are at least eleven dimensions. Most of us only consider the three dimensions. Most people will never bother to research for Truth, even about God. Truth about the Caul or Veil and the relationship to born again Christians is truth that I seek. I trust the revelation of God the Holy Spirit.

BEHEMOTH! I have to share with you my story about Behemoth that is mentioned in Job 40:15-24. For absolutely no reason that I can think of, except the Holy Spirit inspired me, I became engrossed with knowing who or what was the character in the Bible with that name? For weeks, maybe months, I asked God to teach me about Behemoth because there was virtually no information on the presumed mythical character. The assumption is that God included Behemoth in the Bible for a reason. God always has a reason because Romans 8:28 is true.

Driving to the Church one day to finish hanging wallpaper in the fellowship hall, I heard the Lord say, "GO!" I knew that Voice. Immediately, I stepped on the gas and speeded off, just as this humongous branch, as big as a small tree, started falling towards me. It hit a telephone pole on its way down, and landed just behind where I drove. Fire dropped from the wires, as God helped me to outrun the sparks that bounced off the wires behind me, again. That was unbelievable, I kept saying; as I abundantly thanked God for God's Grace that overwhelmed me. A split-second delay on my part to obey God's Voice would have spelled tragedy, probably even death for me.

I arrived at the Church shortly thereafter, unlocked the door to the sanctuary, and turned off the alarm. That spring-day was picture perfect, which made that branch falling even more strange. There was no wind disturbance. The atmosphere was calm. No one else was at the Church, and that made the day even more suitable to get the work done. I unloaded the car and locked myself inside. Still thanking and praising God for goodness and mercy, I laid out the day's redecorating project.

All of a sudden, I heard this thud against the glass door. I eased over to it as a precaution to see what that was that made such a loud, ominous sound. Shock and disbelief engulfed me, and I could not believe what I saw. Like something from a horror movie, the most hideous, ancient looking animal greeted me from the other side of the glass.

Startled to the core, I stood behind the wall and peeped to figure out what in the world was that, and from where did the beast come. As old as the animal was, there was no way it could have gotten up to the door since the time that I brought the equipment inside. The thing looked like a cross between a small horse and a very tall, shaggy dog. I was petrified and trapped; but I did not dare leave without finishing the project. Besides, how could I make my way out of the kitchen door to my car without it seeing me? On the next peep, I saw that the animal was laying down, across the doorway. I would never be able to get out of there, I thought as God led me to pray, ever so calmly. When I looked again, in a few minutes, the animal was gone. That was crazy! Where did it go? I should have been able to spot it walking away. I could not.

"BEHEMOTH", God said. God the Holy Spirit began to teach

me. In a series of one liners God said, "A John the Baptist spirit prepares the way for the entrance of the Spirit of the Lord. Behemoth waddles in the paths that lead believers to a place of blessedness. Beware of the spirit of behemoth that will hinder you. The behemoth spirit is there to intimidate the sons and daughters of God and render them ineffective."

God the Holy Spirit revealed to me that the spirit of behemoth is a dark spirit that is basically harmless. It just waddles in the way to intimidate, distract, and block the blessings of God's sons and daughters through fear and unbelief. Because behemoth blocks the way, we fear; and we are prevented from doing what God told us to do or receive. Behemoth is satan's counterfeit spirit who obstructs the flow of blessings. Just as Mark 1:3 describes, John the Baptist was born and called to prepare the way of the Lord, the behemoth spirit petrifies us and prevents us from moving forward in the plan and purpose of God. God the Holy Spirit defines the way we should go in the Word of God and through direct conversation with us. Listen!

Access to the supernatural knowledge of God is available to us as daughters and sons of God. We must stay open to receive what God has available to us. The range of Godly knowledge and power are limitless. My mind is blown every time God permits me to consider any aspect of God's knowledge or my Christian experience, including childhood. God gave revelation and knowledge to a child like me. Guard and guide our children. God sends revelation through them that have purpose.

We block our own way, like Behemoth, through disobedience, slothfulness, and fear. What would happen if the spiritually gifted children of God really operated in those Gifts? What if, in these last days, God the Holy Spirit desires to give to God's skilled and knowledgeable daughters and sons, greater truths ?

Chapter 15
Oh God!
What Does This Veil Mean?

Matthew 27:51 - "And, behold, the veil of the temple was rent in twain from the top to the bottom; and the earth quaked and the rocks were split;"

Remember some of the truths from the Ordination sermon? God rocks our world. God puts rocks in our world. Remember also that Jesus is absolute Light. Jesus is absolute Righteousness. Jesus is absolute Love. Jesus is absolute Glory. God the Holy Spirit convinces me that there is truth that God reveals about "the Veil" or "Caul Birth" that relates to all born again Christians. If we accept the truth, that truth empowers us at a totally different dimension. That subject matter or other dimension of "knowing" may be the reason God had to write this book in the first place. Interest in the Veil or Caul totally consumed my thoughts when God the Holy Spirit led me to embrace what God shared.

The pursuit of the knowledge about the Veil or Caul commenced rather aggressively because I wanted to know what the Veil or Caul means to our Christian faith. Most Christians would benefit from the fortification of our knowledge and understanding of the blessings to which we have access when the Veil of the Temple was torn from the bottom to the top at the Crucifixion. (Matthew 27:51; Mark 15:38) There are far more blessings of wisdom, revelation, and power that we can acquire about all truth, as a result of our continuous Christian growth in the Holy Spirit. Are we shallow in our Christian faith? Will we move beyond the Veil of the Temple to the quiet, majestic, ethereal place of the Holiest of Holies? The Crucifixion of Jesus Christ, the Messiah King, gives the born again sons and daughters of God access to that realm of the supernatural at all times.

As God the Holy Spirit helps me to know and understand what the Caul or Veil for Caul Births means, I went before God to receive a Word of Knowledge. The enemy's attempt counterfeit or sabotage the information about the Veil or Caul suggests its importance and threat to the kingdom of darkness. God gave me a major breakthrough in revelation as I slept one night. The experience was a quiet, soft move of God, after I wrote most of what comes before in reference to the Veil. Answers from God were diligently sought after. God gave me instructions. I asked God. God answered. This is how the revelation proceeded, and is intended for all who will hear.

One night in a dream, God said: "Behind the Veil lies your difference. (We won't really know what that is until we move.) The difference is who God the Holy Spirit recreates and calls you to be. The difference is your individual uniqueness that can only be discovered and embraced apart from the crowd, the noise, and the error messages of daily life. The pursuit of that difference that I created in you must be persistent while you sojourn in the earth. Behind the Veil is the solitary place where the natural being must be re-born to be the spiritual being that I created and called!"

WOW! Mind you, this revelation was given over the course of a few hours. I awake each morning at 3:00 a.m., and when awakened that morning, I wrote what God the Holy Spirit helped me to remember. The answer I sought was given, and more would be revealed about the Veil and our Christian lives. As the research about the Veil continued, it was evident pretty quickly that the search for truth about it would reveal limited information, at best, from a secular perspective. From a Christian perspective, information is alarmingly close to non-existent. I was led to two scriptures. It is written:

Psalm 139:14 - "I will praise thee; for I am fearfully and wonderfully made: marvelous are thy works; and that my soul knoweth right well."

Do you want to know what is amazingly powerful and so far beyond our comprehension at the same time? We are not just created differently. We are fearfully and wonderfully made, and every individual detail about us, every single one of us. Reread Psalm 139:14, and marvel at the thought that God knew every member of our body before God formed the bodies or created us.
Our souls know something we do not. The labyrinth of God's amazing design within each human being is beyond our full-scope of comprehension. Medical science constantly discovers new details about the human body, and how the multiple systems work together in a miraculous way to maintain life. It is written:

Colossians 1:15-17 – "Who is the image of the invisible God, the firstborn of every creature: for by Him were all things created, that are in heaven, and that are in earth, visible and invisible, whether they be thrones, or dominions, or principalities, or powers: all things were created by him, and for him: and He is before all things, and by him all things consist."

The Veil of Veronica must be considered. From my point of

view, Veronica's emergence during the Crucifixion of Jesus is very significant, though she is not recorded in the Bible. We recall that Luke 2:36-38 tells us that Anna was the prophetess, the woman, who entered the Temple at the precise, divinely designated moment when Mary and Joseph brought Jesus to the Temple. Veronica enters the Crucifixion by Divine interjection.. Anna went from the Temple to tell the good news that the Messiah has come. Anna, a woman, was the FIRST person to proclaim that the Savior has come. In essence, that is all the Gospel really is – to tell the world that Jesus Christ, the Holy and Divine Savior, has come.

Mary Magdalene served with Jesus during His earthly ministry. John 19-20 relays the details of her presence at the Cross, until Jesus was placed in Joseph of Arimathea's new tomb. She was the FIRST Apostle to see, communicate, and interact with Jesus after the Resurrection. Jesus sent her to run from the tomb to the other disciples to tell them Jesus is risen. Jesus told Mary Magdalene to go quickly and tell His disciples, as Dr. Hicks delineated so magnificently in the Ordination sermon. With the same divine precision, God includes Veronica of Jerusalem, another woman, to have a significant role in the Crucifixion events. Veronica was there, on the scene, at the appointed time, for the God ordained purpose to hand Jesus her sweat cloth.. The Crucifixion changed the course of human history forever. Other than Jesus Himself, only the women were prominent.

Only in very recent times in the history of Christianity is the role of women who are included in the Bible considered. Even lesser known is Veronica of Jerusalem, who some people mischaracterize. Other people do not know that she existed; and still other people treat Veronica as insignificant to the horrible process. As Jesus carried the Cross along the streets of Jerusalem that were later called the Via Dolorosa, Veronica wiped Jesus' face with her veil, or sweat cloth which is known in Latin as the Sudarium. An imprint of the Messiah's face remains on that linen cloth, to this day. That Sudarium became known as the Veil of Veronica or the Veronica. The image is yet preserved, and the Catholic Church authenticated that Veil. Anyone who has ever ironed linen fabric knows how delicate that fabric is. The fact that an image burned into the fabric without obliterating it is a Miraculous phenomenon. I say that God the Holy Spirit photographed Jesus, and left the evidence that is yet debated. God the Holy Spirit energizes my spirit, as we lift the Word of Knowledge about the Sudarium or Veil of Veronica.

In the Hebrew or Jewish religion, the High Priest went into the Holiest of Holies within the Tabernacle to make Atonement for sin, once a year. The Veil of the Temple separated the outer court from the inner court or the Holiest of Holies. When Jesus was crucified, the Veil of the Temple was split in two, from the top to the bottom, according to Matthew 27:51, Mark 15:38, and Luke 23:45. No natural phenomenon or human could have been involved in the rending of the Veil. The sheer weight of the Veil would have made that fete impossible. God moved supernaturally to tear the Veil or curtain.

Spiritually, through the power of God the Holy Spirit, that splitting of the Veil grants all Born Again Christians access to the spiritual Holiest of Holies. As the daughters and sons of God, the Crucifixion of Jesus makes direct access to God possible. We are born again into the Royal Priesthood, and therefore we go directly to God for ourselves. God manifested the invisible through the visible. Spiritually, all born again Christians have direct, personal access to that sacred place in the Holiest of Holies.

The Gospel of John 8:12 declares that Jesus is the Light of the world. Further, that verse declares that those who follow Jesus shall not walk in darkness, but shall have the Light of Life. May I call to your attention that Jesus is the Absolute Light, and the power which was within Jesus, etched His image onto the Veil of Veronica before the Crucifixion, without destroying the Veil. That same power etched the image of Jesus onto the Shroud of Turin.

Jesus Resurrected with All-Power, as He tells us in Matthew 28:18. Likewise, that same power of God the Holy Spirit dwells within us, without destroying us. Much debate continues over the authenticity of the image on the Shroud of Turin, also. I prefer to say that the radiant Light who is Jesus took a photo of Himself, again, so we who believe in the Resurrection by faith have tangible evidence to look upon that reflects the unbelievable range of Jesus's power. Jesus, the Logos, left His image on the Veil of Veronica and the Shroud of Turin. Light moves at a speed of 186,000 miles per second. How fast does the Light of Christ move?

I believe that people who are "Born Behind the Veil" or Caul Births are visible evidence, though rare, that Born-again Christians have invisible access to the unlimited power of God to see, know, and do the Will of God. Born-again Christians have access to the same supernatural power, knowledge, sight, and insight, to do greater works than Jesus, as God the Holy Spirit leads us. Through the power of God the Holy Spirit, we acknowledge and use the authority that God gives us to do the Will of God. The evidence shows that born-again Christians use only a dismal amount of the knowledge, power, and energy to which we have access. Technically, all born-again Christians should live in the power of knowing beyond the Veil. We have unlimited access.

Like the Gifting of Caul Bearers, born again Christians who live beyond the Veil, have access to that place of God's abundant love, revelation, power, and peace. We are competent to discern the will of God from that Holy place. A sense of eternity is experienced when we commune with God Beyond the Veil, in the Holiest of Holies, as the Royal Priesthood of God. Jesus is our High Priest, after the Order of Melchizedek, according to Hebrews 7:13-17. There, in that quiet, undisturbed, ethereal, place is the Presence of God. That indeed is God's special, empowering place where we give birth to God's unique creations through the power of God the Holy Spirit. Many will remain outside of the blessedness because of their refusal to relinquish sin, carnal thoughts and actions. It is written:

Numbers 12:6 – "And He (God) said, Hear now my words: If there be a prophet among you, I the Lord will make myself known unto him in a vision, and will speak unto him in a dream."

There are strange ways through which God communicates with God's prophets, prophetesses, and Born-Again Christians who are birthed Beyond the Veil. One of the strangest ways that God communicates is the medium of visions. Because visions are a part of life for Christians who are Born-Again, Beyond the Veil, and because visions are so much a part of my own life, God the Holy Spirit led me through an examination of them to provide some God-inspired insight.

A vision is a panoramic, visual, spiritual transmission from God the Holy Spirit that is designed in eternity and revealed to us at Kairos - God's appointed time. God makes the distinction between the vision and dreams in Numbers 12:6. Unlike a dream, a vision has different dimensions and a realism about it that distinguishes it from a dream, though there are strong similarities and connections. Through the years, the visions that God gave me tended to consist of shades, shadows, color, height, width, and clarity that added depth of perception to the visions' quality.

Through dreams and visions, born again Christians have direct access to revelation or additional divine knowledge from God, through the power of God the Holy Spirit. The "knowing" is often experienced through non-verbal communications that is powerful, direct, and specific. We are spiritual beings. God specializes in bringing to pass the visions and dreams that God gives to us in the first place. We must be obedient, read God's Holy Word, and respond as God directs with gracefulness and humility.

Caul Bearers remind us of all the supernatural power of God the Holy Spirit to which we have access. The ripped Veil of the Temple reminds us as daughters and sons of God that we have unrestricted access to the Authority and Power of Almighty God. People who are Caul Births or Born Beyond the Veil physically are granted special gifts and talents, very much like John the Baptist, who possessed God the Holy Spirit from birth. And yes, like John the Baptist, we who are Caul Bearers may be described as weird by those who are less informed. God reminds us that all born again, Holy Spirit-filled Christians possess the same supernatural ability. When we must embrace what God gives us and use our Gifts of God the Holy Spirit. God refines our Gifts for the Kingdom purpose for which the Gifts were give. We receive more.

For me, people who are Born-Again Christians and receive the anointing of God the Holy Spirit already possess the tremendous Power to do the greater works of Jesus Christ, as He promised. We are Gifted from Rebirth, with precious powers from God that God uses through us. We use the Gifts of God the Holy Spirit for the Kingdom purpose for which they are intended. Live in the power of God the Holy Spirit, beyond the Veil. God the Holy Spirit has legitimate power to remove us from the fringes of the God-life to actively engage in God's divine plan.

Chapter 16
OH GOD!
The Seed is Authentic and Organic!

I Corinthians 2:9 - "But as it is written, Eye hath not seen, nor ear heard, nor ear heard, neither have entered into the heart of man, the things which God hath prepared for them that love Him."

Love God! Love God's seed. Appropriate care, nurturing, and attention to detail are required for the seed throughout the seed's development and maturation. The seed that God the Holy Spirit fertilizes is in us to birth what God ordains to come through us, though the seed does not belong to us. The children that we birth into the world do not belong to us. They belong to God. The children simply come through us. Likewise, the visions and dreams that God gives us do not belong to us or the results when they materialize. The visions and dreams come to us, to come through us; and are a continuing part of God's larger, progressively revealed, eternal plan.

We must be protective and effective stewards of our portion of the visions and dreams which are a part of God's gestation process, and eternal plan for reproduction through us. Visions and dreams tell us portions of the complete story that God the Holy Spirit makes clear to us at the appointed time. Stay ready to receive revelation from God.

As the sons and daughters of God, we are neither trespassers nor intruders in God's Divine plan the way I felt as a student at UGA. God has a special seat reserved for us in the Kingdom. Ephesians 2:6 makes the truth clear that God raises us up to sit in the heavenly places, right now. There, God welcomes us and our conversations with our Loving, All-Powerful God. That is why worry and fear, which come from the enemy, are so unnecessary and Romans 8:28 is such great consolation and inspiration for our journey. We rehearse this scripture, and all the verses of scripture, in our spirit, gently and continually, as God the Holy Spirit leads us to them. Prayer and the Word of God are the supernatural water and food for the seed through which God provides the increase. God is Absolute Power!

The seed that God the Holy Spirit fertilizes is both authentic and organic. An authentic seed has an unquestioned origin. The origin or source of the seed proves itself to be authentic, and the seed speaks for its own authenticity. We know from whence the seed came. All the markings of authenticity are present. The old adage that "the apple doesn't fall far from the tree" is true. No greater authentication of the seed is necessary. The seed of the apple reproduces "after its kind", as Genesis 1:24 commands. Every single apple and the trees from which they come authenticate the original seed and all subsequent apples. The authenticity of the seed goes all the way back to the beginning of creation. Everything about us should authenticate us as the daughters and sons of God. Hallelujah! It is written:

Genesis 1:11 - "And God said, let the earth bring forth grass, the herb yielding seed, and the fruit tree yielding fruit after his kind, whose seed is in itself, upon the earth, and it was so."

Through natural processes, an organic seed breeds, propagates, or reproduces itself from the original seed. An organic seed is derived from living matter which supports the seed's continuing existence and growth. The seed naturally receives and accepts what it needs for life and maturation from that which gives life. Nothing artificial or synthetic is introduced into the seed's existence. The organic seed draws what it needs from naturally recurring substances.

Likewise, God the Holy Spirit supernaturally prepares the heart to be fertile ground to receive the authentic seed of faith, and provides what the seed of faith needs, organically, through the Word of God. God the Holy Spirit fertilizes the seed for reproduction. "Be ye Holy for I am Holy", says the Lord. Holiness comes only from the Lord, and it is organic and authentic. Those who possess the power of God the Holy Spirit embrace true holiness as authentic and organic. That is what the true Church of Jesus Christ seeks in this hour of history

God said to me: "The greater works for which I have anointed you and the Miracle working power that I assigned to follow you will not operate in a shallow places or with shallow people who don't trust Me. Go forward. Come out from among them and be separate for Me. My grace is sufficient for you. My Strength (Power) is made perfect in your weakness."

Miracles happen when we profess and confess that we need a Miracle from God. We must believe the Miracle will happen, against all odds and despite conditions. "Have faith in God", as Mark 11:22 instructs us. Miracles always point back to God as the only Source of the Miracle. So, that means that the Miracles are authentic and organic works of God; and we know them to be so. Seed of doubt are never permitted.

Sarah and Abraham in Genesis 18 - 21, Hannah and Elkanah in

I Samuel 1, Manoah and his wife in Judges 13, Elizabeth and Zechariah in Luke 1 are our Biblical examples of how God acts through people to fulfill God's plan. The births of their sons were Miraculous, authentic, and organic. God's work through these phenomenal characters inspired me as a woman whose heart desire was to be a mother. Miracles are for us and demonstrate the unlimited extremities of God's love for us. For God, Miracles are simply more of God's activated thought toward us that supersedes all obstacles.

From the beginning of my preaching ministry until now, I never debated or argued with anyone for any reason about my call to preach the Gospel because I am a woman. After all God brought George and me through, how ludicrous, ridiculous, and disrespectful to God would that be? Like Mary Magdalene, I took the yoke of the Lord Jesus Christ, the Messiah King, upon my spirit, soul and body to learn of Him, as Matthew 11:29 instructs.

Oh, do not get the facts twisted. There were and always will be people, male and female, who are opposed to preachers who are female. Women outnumber men in most congregations, still, in the Church. Ungodly action, including jealousy and envy, cause women to resent other women, and support pastors who deny women the opportunity to be licensed and/or ordained. What I have observed ever since my Ordination is those congregations continue to stop growing and to die who have perpetually denied preachers who are women the opportunity to preach. From where I stand, the amazing preachers who GOD calls, GOD also qualifies, as Dr. Hicks use to say, male and female. God's choice has nothing to do with the preferences of individuals. The bastion of male dominance over women in a congregation breeds its own demise without warning. It is written:

I John 4:1 - "Beloved, believe not every spirit, but try the spirits whether they are of God: because many false prophets are gone out into the world."

God the Holy Spirit gives the preachers that God calls, females and males, God's authority and ability to proclaim the Salvation of Jesus Christ; and to powerfully engage in spiritual warfare. Our job, females and males, is to discern the will and presence of God, in every situation. One thing for sure, God the Holy Spirit will always permit us to discern if the spirit who speaks about God or the Word of God to us, or about us is a Godly spirit. In the spirit, we simply ask: "Are you the spirit who believes that Jesus is the Son of God?" The spirit will either confirm or deny Christ. Silence is not of God. We only receive Godly spirits.

When Reverend Dr. Marvis P. May left Metropolitan, he became the Senior Pastor of the Macedonia Baptist Church in Baltimore, Maryland. May was on staff as the Assistant to the Senior Minister at Metropolitan when I came aboard as Youth Director. For a while, he and I were the only full-time ministry staff, in addition to Dr. Hicks and Ms. Drusilla Boddie who was the Church secretary. I was devastated when my first Comrade left because we had done so much great ministry together, and our families were close.

For his last sermon as staff, Reverend May preached the familiar and powerful sermon, "The Macedonian Call", from Acts 16:6-10. A true man of God and extraordinary preacher, he performed the most incredible works in ministry, the way Jesus mandated. May served the needs of the people, especially the elderly; the sick and shut-in members; people in need; and the homeless. He was an avid reader who possessed the unusual ability to interpret Bible-based truth, exegetical research, as well as modern and contemporary thought with profound clarity. Generally, he preached powerful and transformational sermons in 15 minutes, or less. He was a rare gift to the Body of Christ.

Dr. May and his children spent many Friday or Saturday evenings at our home, as they watched wrestling with my husband and children. My only participation in those events, basketball, or football games, was to prepare meals for the families that were voraciously consumed; which brought them and me great joy. We had tremendous respect for each other as Christians and parents. In fact, I was pleasantly surprised when he and our Director of Church Music stopped by my office one day to share with me one of the most treasured compliments that I ever have received. That day, they literally stopped by to share with me that they thought that I fully embodied what a woman of God, wife, and mother should embody. I was humbled enormously, and grateful for the very generous comment. However, Dr. May did not believe in "women preachers".

From Dr. May, during one of our countless Theological conversations, I accepted the idea that God calls us out of our humanity, and in spite of it. Strangely enough, the Sunday that May preached the farewell sermon from Acts 16:9 about the Apostle's Paul's vision of a man pleading to him to come over to Macedonia to help them, I knew my time was up. I had to preach. Interestingly enough, though I had never paid the appropriate attention to the text in context, following the story of Paul's Macedonian Call, is the story of Lydia. Lydia was the wealthy woman, a seller of the expensive color purple, and entrepreneur who helped open the way for Christianity to enter Europe with the other women. God used Paul and the women, together.

Shortly after Dr. May moved to Baltimore, I confessed my call to preach. May drove over to Metropolitan from Baltimore to give me his blessing on my confession. He said, "Miller, I don't believe God calls women to preach. But, I believe God called you to preach." I thanked him and said that was a good start. The next step was that he attended my Ordination, three years later. That was huge for Dr. May; and his presence blessed me, immensely.

When our family relocated to Atlanta, we planted The Messiah's Temple Christian Ministries. Some Pastors who said they would help us to do so, did not. As a matter of fact, they totally ignored my calls once I arrived back home. Nevertheless, the same way that God the Holy Spirit did to establish everything Pamoja at UGA, and the Metropolitan Baptist Church Youth Ministries, the Holy Spirit designed our Church. After one year in existence, we chartered The Messiah's Temple Christian Ministries in Austell, Georgia, a suburb of Atlanta.

God's extraordinary grace permitted Reverend Dr. Marvis P. May, Reverend Dr. Casey and LeeDonna Kimbrough, Reverend Dr. William and Lynn Harris, Reverend H. Wesley and Doris Wiley, and Reverend Patrick Young to be present for our two services at Charter Day. Their wives, families, and some members of the Churches where they pastored, were with us. The Shekinah Glory drenched us in worship and fellowship, the entire weekend.

When Dr. May transitioned to glory, unexpectedly, on November 24, 2007, I was beyond devastated. We were in the process of making plans for me to preach at Macedonia Baptist Church. His decision to do that was huge. Needless to say, many were shocked when his beloved son, M.J., granted me the honor to close his casket. I invited our Comrades, and other Clergy who had served at Metropolitan to participate with me, "a preacher who happens to be a lady." We circled his body in tears. The tribute that the homeless people made as they came in the church together, walked past the casket to pay their last respect made my heart overflow with love and gratitude. As many Homegoings as we have seen, we never saw such a tribute from homeless people.

Boldly confident that Jesus always sees me, and that Jesus will always see about me, I choose to follow the example of the Apostle Mary Magdalene to do ministry for Jesus Christ. For me, her example teaches us to:

- Stay close to Jesus through the power of God the Holy Spirit.
- Trust God's call on your life.
- Be bold to do the Kingdom work.
- Ignore the detractors and naysayers.
- Watch the Miracles flow.
- Stay present to the end.
- FEAR NOT!

That summer morning in that high chair when I burned myself and encountered Jesus forever impacts my life. . That fire roasting summer day outside of the Atlanta Public Library waiting for George, I determined within myself to always wait on the Lord. Those angels that I encountered at UGA, and all the experiences of my life, permanently endowed me with faith and trust in God that I needed to do everything God assigns to me. I am hopelessly life-locked to the Triune God. God sent God's son to die for us. We commit to live our lives for Jesus. It is written:

Job 13:15 - "Though He slay me, yet will I trust Him..."

It is still true. God uses whom God chooses; and God chooses who God uses. The Biblical evidence indicates that God calls families to Kingdom service, as well as single women and men, like the Apostle Mary Magdalene and the Apostle Paul. I know for sure that God called our family which is why satan worked so hard to steal from us; to kill us; and to destroy us. God often reminds me of the day God confirmed our family's call to do ministry to which God assigned our hands.

One night, as I drove home from Bible Study in tears, God and I talked about some of the challenges of rearing four children, and starting a Church ministry as a Pastor-Preacher who is a woman, in the Bible belt. Never have I regretted doing what God told me to do, but I cried out to God for God's revelation and my understanding.

As I drove alone, on that very dark stretch of roadway, I suddenly had the most amazing, overwhelming epiphany. With a flood of tears streaming down my face, such that I could hardly see, I suddenly realized that this steep and winding road to our home, around the mountain from which I heard God speak Caleb's words to me that day, was the same path that I had dreamed about since childhood. That road was the same road that I could see far in the distance from the front porch of our home-house in Atlanta where I grew up. Through the years, when we came home to visit Atlanta, I would sit on the front porch and look at that road, especially when the leaves were fallen. I SAW THAT ROAD.

The branches from the trees on either side of the road met in the middle. I knew that was the same road I had dreamed about all of my life. I was shocked and knew that God showed that to me, that night. Then, I heard God speak.

God said, "I called them, too." God called our family. Amen! That was what the enemy tried to kill. God is VICTORY. Tears of joy and thanksgiving flooded my soul.

237

Chapter 17
Thank God!
The Father Is Not Impotent!

John 15:8 - "Herein is My Father glorified, that ye bear much fruit; so shall ye be my disciples."

This preacher was pregnant with two sons and two daughters whose births are a physical anomaly; a Church; and an abundance of ministries to others. We are emphatically grateful to God that our sons and daughters serve God, and model their Christian faith as a result of what they lived as life choices. Within them is more seed to reproduce after its kind, as they have begun to do, already.

There is NO DOUBT! Our first born son should be an alcoholic because of the volume of wine I had to drink to bring him into the world, alive. The unfathomable way that Grace spared him, keeps us in a state of humble gratitude. All the outstanding research that Dr. Fabro presented and supported with statistical data was Miraculously defied with his prescription of wine for us. Only God could have arranged for Dr. Fabro's life to intersect ours in such a way that Miracles made the impossible births realities.

God's Grace permitted George to graduate from Morehouse College. On graduation day, he marched out from the ceremony at Morehouse, and up to the pulpit to preach at the Messiah's

Temple Christian Ministries Church. Dr. H. Beecher Hicks, Jr. married Cheri Alexander and George after George earned the Master of Divinity Degree from Emory University - Candler Theological Seminary. Dr. Casey Kimbrough, Senior Pastor of Mt. Carmel Baptist Church in Charlotte, North Carolina, conducted George's Ordination Council and Service at Mt. Carmel. Similar to the precaution that Dr. Hicks took against potential challenges to my Ordination, I took the same precautions because his Pastor is a woman and his Mother.

George worked through some ostracism at Morehouse from other students who were sons of Pastors, and other young men who planned to become clergy. They did not believe in "women preachers". He was deliberately not included in "the group" or any Theological discussions because of me. Our ministry is non-denominational. Therefore, those male students, influenced most likely by their fathers who were Pastors, did not consider our Church or George as legitimate or viable. These young men of a new generation perpetuated the same stereotypical behavior in the Bible Belt that their fathers before them practiced. The practices of discrimination against preachers and Pastors who are women is an indication of cowardly insecurities, while the men get women in their Churches to do their bidding like a slave master. That bias was and is wrong. That Sunday after Ordination, I preached at the 11:00 a.m. service at Mt. Carmel; then our family and church family, drove back from Charlotte. The storms through which we drove were the start of Hurricane Katrina, though we did not know that.

Reverend George C. Miller, III became the Senior Pastor of Messiah's Temple Christian Ministries, the Church our family helped to plant with him as a teenager. Later, he accepted the position of Executive Pastor at the historic Tabernacle Baptist

Church in Augusta, Georgia. His friend and brother from their Seminary days at Candler, Reverend Dr. Charles Goodman, is Senior Pastor. While at Tabernacle for eight years, Pastor George earned his M.B.A. Degree. Currently, he is the Senior Pastor of the historic Elim Baptist Church in Augusta, Georgia; and a Doctoral Candidate at the Interdenominational Theological Center in Atlanta. Initially, before moving his family to Augusta, he commuted three hours, each way, from Augusta to Atlanta, daily, for a year. He learned ministry commitment from a lady.

As a teenager, George was grieved when we moved from Fairfax, Virginia because he was forced to leave his lifelong friends, and Cheri Alexander behind at Metropolitan. Cheri was the girl he "church-dated". Three years later, God brought Cheri to college at Clark-Atlanta University, where she earned her B.A. degree. She is a Licensed Minister, who is currently in two Master Degree Programs - one in math education and one in Theological education. Together, Pastor George and Minister Cheri Miller parent four marvelous sons. All of them, together, bring the love of Christ to their community, city, state and assigned locations.

When our sons were growing up, I often remarked that if they went through life together, they would be a perfect person. One had qualities that the other did not have, so they complimented each other, well. Remember the instruction from Dr. Benjamin Mays? "If it is a male child, send "them" to Morehouse." Though George and John E. Miller were born 13 months apart, they were pretty much reared as twins. They started Morehouse a year apart, but both of them earned Bachelor Degrees in Business Administration, the same year.

When John and George walked in with the other Morehouse men that morning, between the storm, to the cadence of African drums, an overflow of silent tears streamed down my face. I could sense God smile at us in our very reverent state of joy over God's Gifts to us. In my heart, I smiled back. Like the loving Father that God is, God permitted John and George to graduate together and march together. I could not believe it. That was God's personal, bonus blessing to me that only God and I would ever understand. On the wall in our home is a photo on a plaque of John as he received his degree. Years later, we spot George in the photo, as he was providentially captured, waiting, watching, and praying for his younger brother, as he received his degree.

John asked me years later if I thought I would ever get back all that I sacrificed as a mother. I told him that though I was not expecting or wanted anything for the honor of rearing our sons and daughters, God gave everything back to me that morning of graduation, and subsequent graduations of our children, and the generations.. He is the baby who survived, in a womb riddled with fibroids that never attached properly.

John earned his M.B.A. from Clark-Atlanta University in 2008. Upon graduation from Morehouse College in 2002, John began a very successful career as a stockbroker and an Investment Consultant for a financial services firm. He greatly engendered clients' trust and commitment, while he delivered a return on their investments. His reputation is that of an astute and very capable manager who is skilled at assessing client needs; and promoting transparency through consistent communication. John is also a Partner and Principal Relationship Manager for Resonant Brands, LLC. He is a determined and focused leader who understands that "relationships matter", and every interaction with people must be valued.

The high spirited entrepreneur transmits the same high energy, quality of care, and concern to the broader Atlanta community. He has held several leadership roles where the key to his success has always been the development of the people with whom he serves. Together, they produced outstanding results. For example, he is a member of the Urban League of Greater Atlanta Young Professionals, where he led as the Sub-Committee Chairman for Personal and Professional Development.

John brings outstanding leadership as a working member of the Board of Directors for The Institute for Christian Discipleship, Inc. (ICD). ICD is a non-profit organization that we birthed the same time that The Messiah's Temple was birthed. It provides high-level spiritual, Christian education services through local and national conferences, workshops in interpersonal development; skills training; family support; and personal empowerment.

Politically, John continuously participates as an organizer and grassroots supporter for various political campaigns. He served as Curriculum Co-Chairman for the New Leaders Council (NLC). NLC is an organization that trains and supports the political entrepreneur of tomorrow. They are the trendsetters, elected officials, and civically-engaged leaders in business and industry that shape the landscape for years to come. John's passion for social justice is activated and chronicled on the tabloids of individual lives. For him, relevant to his Christian faith is the empowerment of children and youth through education; the empowerment of the disenfranchised through political action; and the empowerment of families through financial education and skills development.

In 2014, Bri Pennie and John were married. John's youngest sibling made a great observation about their courtship and marriage. Victoria said, "John finally found a female version of himself." Bri graduated Magna Cum Laude from Georgia Southern University where she earned the B.S. Degree. She earned the M.B.A. with honors, concentrating in Marketing, from

Mercer University. Bri is Founder and Principal Strategist for Resonant Brands. Together, they travel nationally and internationally for fun and to negotiate business; skydive; rock climb; ride their motorcycles; and other adventurers. Among their greatest adventures is parenting their first born son. They too have a marriage that represents Christ and His Church.

The trauma of Mikah Miller's birth should have adversely affected her both physically and mentally, even now. It did not, in any manner. God is Grace. We really should have sued the Anesthesiologist who talked about her date, while she incorrectly administered the epidural that almost killed our baby and me. We did not. God was there for us in an immeasurably powerful way, despite the fact that the enemy attempted to wipe us out. God's Abundant Grace left no room for me to sue, in spite of the fact that the doctor was unquestionably negligent.

Mikah graduated from Tuskegee University in Tuskegee, Alabama, where she earned the Bachelor of Arts Degree with a major in Psychology. The Master of Arts Degree was earned at Argosy University; and she plans to pursue the Doctorate. Mikah has an outstanding track record as a Behavioral Health Practitioner, who is passionately dedicated to helping people build or rebuild their lives. She works from the core competencies of individual counselling; child and adolescent behavior modification; marriage therapy; PTSD/trauma therapy; Veterans Counselling; substance abuse/addiction counselling; and crisis intervention.

While at Devereux Advanced Behavioral Health, Mikah was chosen as Employee of the Year. She was a Behavioral Health Specialist at Mercy Care which also serves our homeless people and people in need. She fondly remembers her early days when our family helped the homeless citizens in Washington, D.C., and people in need in Atlanta. Mikah credits her experiences in Street Ministries and watching her Mother work with the diverse populations as the most significant influence in her career choice to be a Behavioral Therapist.

She founded and manages her very effective private Behavioral Therapist practice, With A Child's Heart, LLC, in three locations in metropolitan Atlanta. Her client base includes children, adolescents, At-Risk youth, and adults. Mikah credits the work she saw God do through me for people in need who were homeless for her career choice. A portion of her interview with *Voyage Atlanta* (voyageatl.com) reads:

"We understand that life's challenges can interrupt or even stunt the emotional maturation of individuals. These challenges cause their perception to be altered, and resentment or grudges to develop. We find those moments in time that truly affect our clients, and then help them to work through them."

As a mother who is single, Mikah successfully parents one son who exudes confidence as a result of her parenting skills. Her Christ-life, her son, her family, and clients are top priorities.

Miraculously born after a ten year gap in George's and my childbearing years, Victoria is our midlife blessing for whom we are well-pleased. She graduated Magna Cum Laude from Georgia State University in 2016, her father's Alma Mater. Graduation was the week of my 65th birthday. With her very successful major in Criminal Justice, it is fitting for our family that we would end our obligation to educate our sons and daughters where George and I began our story almost 50 years earlier! God is amazing and in our details!

Victoria began her professional career with the Criminal Justice

Coordinating Council, Grants and Policy Division, as an intern, while a student at Georgia State. Subsequently, she received a full time position. She is a proven, balanced, and assertive leader whose background is evidence of her ability to make clearly productive decisions in a fast paced environment. Victoria is a wonderful, creative Millennial who is a critical thinker. She applies that skill, as well as intellectual curiosity and abilities, to any situation or challenge imposed. She is an astute and focused individual who provides cutting edge solutions to complex situations. She begins her pursuit of the Master's Degree in Public Policy that will lead to her acquisition of the Ph.D. degree.

While her Dad and I took total responsibility for rearing Victoria, she technically grew up with five parents, three of whom were her siblings. Her Dad and Deacon Odean Horne prayed for us to have another baby. God answered. When Victoria was born in 1993, God gave me the title for this book - *Oh God! My Preacher Is Pregnant!* God the Holy Spirit poured so many thoughts into my spirit, I did not know how I would ever get them all said and done.

As I muse with God the Holy Spirit, I ponder the delicate balance between life and giving birth to new life. Unlike other things and situations in which we are involved, there is only one chance to get 40 weeks of pregnancy, and subsequent delivery of the baby right. A mother does not get a "do over" after birth. Likewise, we aim for excellence in the fulfillment of all dreams and visions. The gates of hell did and do press against us! As God promises, they do not and shall not prevail against us in the pressing. The vignettes of life are endless. We must make sure that our dreams, visions, and vignettes are God blessed through prayer and obedience.

The ebb and flow of our existence here on earth challenges us to remember the Providence of Almighty God as our assurance of what God will bring to pass. Be patient. We are here as breathing, viable, humans because God patiently permitted us to enter the earth realm, at a specific time, for a specific duration, and specific purpose. Just as every wave of the ocean is connected and then merged together with ever other wave, we are reminded that everything is connected to everything else, until or unless the connection is broken, intentionally or unintentionally! The umbilical cord that connects the mother and the child in the womb must ultimately be cut so that the child may exist to adulthood and old age, independently, under the watchful Eye of the Creator God. We patient embrace the value of each other's existence.

I finally wear the ecclesiastical robe as a loose garment, lest it become a lead overcoat. I finally acknowledge that I am a Caul Bearer, Born Behind the Veil, who shares the knowledge from God the Father, God the Son, and God the Holy Spirit. The born again daughters and sons of God are birthed behind the Veil through the Power of God the Holy Spirit! The crossroads and the milestones changed me! I will show them my scars! Thank God!

Thank God, the Father is not impotent! What God desires to birth is always birthed, despite humanity or human conditions. Thank God for power, knowledge, wisdom, revelation, and understanding that God reveals to Kingdom people who are ready to receive what God is willing to give! God is Present! Thank God for Calvary! Thank God for Pentecost! Because God is not impotent, God births the impossible. It is written:

Romans 8:31 – "What shall we then say to these things? If God be for us, who can be against us?"

THANK GOD!

…About the Author!

Reverend Nawanna Lewis Miller is married to her high school sweetheart, George C. Miller, Jr., since 1972. They are native Atlantans, who lived in Fairfax, Virginia for almost 20 years before returning to live in the metropolitan Atlanta suburbs. Together, they are the phenomenally blessed parents to two adult sons; four adult daughters; and the grandparents to six grandsons.

She is the author of three books: **Angels in My Room; Cruising the Cosmos;** and **Heal the Hurt: Live the Victory.** Pastor Miller is the Founding Pastor of The Messiah's Temple Christian Ministries; Director and Lead Teacher of The Institute for Christian Discipleship, Inc., since 1995; Visionary Leader for Hannah's Hope Family Life Ministries; and other ministries.

This author writes as a winner who wins, victoriously, through God the Holy Spirit, in her life, despite many odds against her doing so. She is one of the first 25 African American graduates of the University of Georgia in Athens, Georgia, where she earned the ABJ Degree in Broadcast Journalism. The M.A. Degree in Organizational Communications was earned from the Graduate School of Arts and Sciences at Howard University in Washington, D.C.; and the M.Div. Degree was earned at the Howard University School of Divinity.

The two upcoming books that God the Holy Spirit writes through Reverend Miller are: **The Glorified Stroke! A Management Consulting Project;** and **B.O.L.O.** She may be contacted through Facebook at The Institute for Christian Discipleship, Inc., or through the website @ icdlearning.com. We thank you for reading. God blesses you.

Oh God! My Preacher is Pregnant!